THE THIRST OF SATAN

George Sterling

THE THIRST OF SATAN

POEMS OF FANTASY AND TERROR

George Sterling

Edited and with an Introducton
by S. T. Joshi

Hippocampus Press

New York

Published by Hippocampus Press
P.O. Box 641, New York, NY 10156.
http://www.hippocampuspress.com

First Edition
1 3 5 7 9 8 6 4 2

ISBN 0-9721644-6-4

Contents

Introduction

In many ways it is unjust to segregate the weird or fantastic poetry of George Sterling (1869–1926) from the rest of his copious poetic output, since Sterling—who, despite his current obscurity, has a valid claim to the title of leading American lyric poet of the twentieth century—never envisioned working in such a vein; even his most "cosmic" work, *The Testimony of the Suns*, he passed off merely as a "'Star' poem,"[1] and perhaps only "A Wine of Wizardry" was consciously intended to inspire terror. Sterling's poetry ran the gamut of subjects—love and death, humanity and society, even politics and war—and only occasionally and incidentally did so in a manner that can in retrospect be termed fantastic. And yet it is clear that Sterling had a clear affinity for fantastic themes—perhaps more so than many other American poets of his time.

Sterling was born in Sag Harbor, Long Island, and educated there and in Maryland, where he studied with the minor poet John Banister Tabb (1845–1909). In 1890 he decided to come to California both to pursue a career—his wealthy uncle, F. C. Havens, was a prosperous businessman in the Bay Area—and to develop his literary gifts. He quickly became acquainted with Joaquin Miller (1837–1913), the flamboyant poet who had gained celebrity in England with the publication of *Songs of the Sierras* (1871). No later than 1896, Sterling became friends with California's Great Cham of Letters, Ambrose Bierce (1842–1914?), who had not only established himself as a prominent short story writer and poet (although he disavowed the latter title), but also was the most

---

1. "[Jack] London wants to criticize my 'Star' poem, but I think I'll wait and hear what you have to say about it." (Sterling to Ambrose Bierce, 4 March 1902; ms., New York Public Library). All manuscript letters by Sterling, Bierce, and Clark Ashton Smith cited in the introduction and commentary are at the New York Public Library unless otherwise indicated.

feared and respected journalist and critic on the West Coast. In his weekly "Prattle" column for the *San Francisco Examiner*, he magisterially settled the fates of the writers, politicians, clergymen, and other hapless beings who fell under his sharp and withering glance. Sterling's first extant letters to Bierce date to 1897, and it was about that time that he began to send his early poems to Bierce. Bierce was impressed to the degree of quoting them in full in some of his columns of 1899, and in 1901 (now transferred to Washington, D.C.) he arranged for the publication of Sterling's "Memorial Day" in the *Washington Post*.

In late 1901 Sterling began work on the poem that would bring him his first taste of fame. *The Testimony of the Suns* elicited immediate enthusiasm from Bierce:

> Where are you going to stop?—I mean at what stage of development? . . . This last beats any and all that went before—or I am bewitched and befuddled. I dare not trust myself to say what I think of it. In manner it is great, but the greatness of the theme!—that is beyond anything.
>
> It is a new field, the broadest yet discovered. . . . The tremendous phenomena of Astronomy have never had adequate poetic treatment, their meaning adequate expression. You must make it your domain. You shall be the poet of the skies, the prophet of the suns. (Bierce to Sterling, 15 March 1902)

In spite of the dates Sterling affixed to the poem (December 1901 for Part I, February 1902 for Part II), he did not complete the poem until May. Bierce made exhaustive marginal notations and comments on the draft, many of which Sterling acknowledged when making subsequent revisions.[2] For many years following, Sterling in his letters to Bierce addressed the older writer as "Master," much to Bierce's consternation and embarrassment; but such was Sterling's great respect for Bierce's wisdom and erudition.

Whether *The Testimony of the Suns* is Sterling's greatest poem is open to question; certainly, it is one of his most impressive. The vibrant depiction of cosmic conflict, although occasionally obscure in sense and diction, is a triumph of the imagination; but Sterling knew that it was not without human significance: "I hope that it will be clear enough to

---

2. Sterling's draft, as annotated by Bierce, was published as *The Testimony of the Suns* (San Francisco: Printed for The Book Club of California by John Henry Nash, 1927).

the intellectual reader that my invocation to the stars is only an allegory of man's search of the universe for the secret of life" (Sterling to Bierce, 3 June 1902). Although Bierce was worried that the second part of the poem would produce a let-down because it might involve a sentimental "human element" that would weaken the force of the cosmic first part, he was relieved when he finally read it: "You did the trick excellently well—got down to earth again without accident" (Bierce to Sterling, 20 June 1902). The fundamental message of that second part appears to be the failure of the human mind to find any "meaning" in the stars aside from the notion of constant struggle, warfare, and ultimate transience. Since the stars themselves will one day perish, what hope can human beings have of staving off oblivion?

The poem was far too long to be published in a magazine, even if Sterling had had a poetic reputation at that time; so he included it in his first book, *The Testimony of the Suns and Other Poems* (1903), published by a San Francisco businessman, W. E. Wood. Shortly thereafter, in 1904, the volume was reprinted by A. M. Robertson, the bookseller and publisher who would issue the majority of Sterling's books during his lifetime. Many copies of that second edition were destroyed in the San Francisco earthquake of 1906, so Robertson reprinted it in 1907.

Sterling continued to send his poems to Bierce for comment and approval. He quoted bits of "A Wine of Wizardry"—which he called "a poem of 'pure imagination'"—in a letter of 2 January 1904; at that time it already included two of its most striking lines:

> The blue-eyed vampire, sated at her feast,
> Smiles bloodily against the leprous moon.

Bierce was not slow to respond, noting that the above lines "give me the shivers. Gee! they're awful!" (Bierce to Sterling, 8 January 1904). By the end of the month the poem was finished. Its "plot," if such it can be called, is simple: the poet drinks a wine that awakens his "Fancy," who ventures on a variety of fantastic voyages, alternately lovely and horrific. (Upton Sinclair, a fervent teetotaller, suggested that the work should have been titled "The Wizardry of Wine.") On occasion the poem descends to mere catalogues of jewelled words and phrases, but on the whole it is a powerful exercise of imagination—a more earthly imagination, certainly, than *The Testimony of the Suns,* but one in which horror and fantasy are inextricably united.

For years Bierce strove to secure the magazine publication of "A Wine of Wizardry." Although not as long as *The Testimony of the Suns,* it was still a long poem, hence not easily saleable; and its exoticism made it doubly difficult to market at a time when an attenuated Victorianism still demanded that poets speak in a reserved and conventional manner. Bierce sanguinely observed, "It is impossible to imagine a magazine editor rejecting that poem" (Bierce to Sterling, 11 May 1904), but that is exactly what happened. *Scribner's, Harper's,* the *Atlantic Monthly, Munsey's,* the *Metropolitan,* the *Bookman,* even *Cosmopolitan* (for which Bierce had begun writing in 1905) all turned it down. Bierce showered abuse upon the editors of these magazines, but perhaps a bit unjustly: the poem's length, its imagery, and the fact that Sterling was by no means a well-known literary figure all militated against its ready acceptance.

Bierce then sent the poem to Herman Scheffauer (an earlier poetic pupil of Bierce's who, much to his own irritation, quickly took second rank as a disciple once Sterling emerged) to market in England, but with no success. Sterling offered it to *Sunset,* a West Coast magazine that had run some of his earlier verse, but to no avail. For a time it looked as if Walter Neale (1873–1933), who in 1909 began issuing Bierce's *Collected Works,* might include it in a magazine he was contemplating, but the magazine was never begun. A. M. Robertson thought of bringing out the poem as a pamphlet in a 500-copy edition on Japanese vellum, but Bierce expressed disapproval of this kind of "limited edition," believing that it would restrict the poem's audience to collectors. Finally, a new editor, Sam Chamberlain, took over at *Cosmopolitan* in the summer of 1907 and expressed a wish to print the poem. Bierce had written an effusive article, "A Poet and His Poem," to run concurrently with "A Wine of Wizardry." Both appeared in the September 1907 issue, and Sterling was paid $100 for the poem.

A firestorm of controversy ensued. Some readers and critics, perhaps offended by Bierce's high praise of the poem, misconstrued his essay and maintained that Bierce believed the poem to be the greatest ever written in America. In fact, much of the incredulity and scoffing to which "A Wine of Wizardry" was subject was a result of two passages in Bierce's essay, the first about *The Testimony of the Suns* ("Of that work I have the temerity to think that in both subject and art it nicks the rock as high as anything of the generation of Tennyson, and a good deal higher than anything of the generation of Kipling"), the second about Sterling in general:

> . . . I steadfastly believe and hardily affirm that George Sterling is a very great poet—incomparably the greatest that we have on this side

of the Atlantic. And of this particular poem I hold that not in a lifetime has our literature had any new thing of equal length containing so much poetry and so little else.[3]

Note carefully what Bierce actually says: Sterling is the greatest *living* American poet, and "A Wine of Wizardry" has more quintessential poetry than any other poem written within Bierce's lifetime. Neither of these statements is, as we can now see, as controversial as Bierce's contemporaries believed. It is a brute fact that American poetry, from the death of Longfellow in 1882 to the emergence of Edwin Arlington Robinson and Robert Frost in the 1920s, was at a particularly low ebb, so that to affirm in 1907 that George Sterling was America's finest living poet was to speak what could very well be the truth. Bierce's second comment is perhaps a bit of an exaggeration, as it seems to give short shrift to Swinburne (a clear influence on Sterling, at least in regard to diction) and the Pre-Raphaelites; but Bierce was not fond of these poets and sincerely believed Sterling to be their superior. Other parts of Bierce's essay—especially when he likens parts of "A Wine of Wizardry" (notably the "blue-eyed vampire" lines) to celebrated passages in Coleridge and Keats—do indeed make one question whether Bierce's fondness for Sterling had gotten the better of his critical judgment.

But the furore over the poem was, as Bierce saw, a product of two quite different elements: first, the fact that very few individuals of his day (and, sadly, of ours) had any true grasp of the essence of poetry, hence could not recognise it when they saw it; and, second, the fact that several of Bierce's enemies were waiting for an opportunity to pay him back in kind for the abuse they had themselves suffered. Accordingly, a variety of hostile, jeering, or supercilious remarks about both Bierce and Sterling began appearing in the Hearst newspapers (notably the *San Francisco Examiner* and the *New York American*) and elsewhere—much of it fostered by Hearst's editors merely as an entertaining nine-days' wonder. Bierce himself relished the fray: in the December 1907 issue of *Cosmopolitan* he published a fiery broadside, "An Insurrection of the Peasantry," in which he took to task all the critics of Sterling and himself, in particular those (such as George Harvey, then editor of *Harper's Weekly*) who had written that "A Wine of Wizardry" had a kind of superfluity of poetic imagination—as if a poem could ever have too much!

---

3. "A Poet and His Poem" and its sequel, "An Insurrection of the Peasantry," are both found in the tenth volume of Bierce's *Collected Works*.

Two years later, A. M. Robertson published Sterling's *A Wine of Wizardry and Other Poems*. The book contains many other fine works aside from the title poem, notably "Three Sonnets on Oblivion," with its emphasis on human transience, and poems on Poe and Bierce, the latter of which Walter Neale reprinted as a broadside. *The House of Orchids* (1911) and *Beyond the Breakers* (1914) also have superb work: "The Black Vulture," one of Sterling's most reprinted poems and a grim portrayal of the all-destroying power of Death; "The Thirst of Satan," whose cosmic imagery is reminiscent of *The Testimony of the Suns;* and "The Ashes in the Sea," a delicate elegy on Nora May French (1881–1907), the young poet who committed suicide in November 1907 while staying at Sterling's cabin in Carmel.

Bierce returned to California for lengthy visits in 1910 and 1912, going with Sterling and some others to Yosemite and other sites; in the summer of 1911 he visited Sterling at Sag Harbor. But the two men were growing apart, and a final split occurred in early 1913. The causes for the end of their friendship are a matter of conjecture, since neither Bierce nor Sterling discussed them in detail. We have only suggestive hints: Sterling's continued adherence to Socialism (as well as his friendship with the fervent Socialist Jack London, whom Bierce disdained) did not sit well with the increasingly conservative satirist; Sterling's involvements with married women (especially one Vera Connolly, about whom Sterling's wife Carrie wrote some poignant letters to Bierce in late 1911) were highly offensive to Bierce's strict sexual morality; and some of Sterling's later poems exhibited frank sexual elements that Bierce did not feel worthy of inclusion in verse. In any case, Bierce had been systematically banishing several of his close colleagues as he made plans in late 1913 to visit Mexico (ostensibly to witness the Mexican Civil War), so perhaps it is not surprising that the greatest of his poetic disciples also would be shown the door.

In early 1911, however, Sterling himself gained the opportunity to become a mentor of a young poetic disciple of his own; for it was then that Clark Ashton Smith, having just celebrated his eighteenth birthday, first wrote to Sterling. Sterling had by this time largely taken over Bierce's function as literary leader of the West Coast, and—especially upon his moving to Carmel in 1905 as the vanguard of a literary colony there—had gathered a group of like-minded colleagues: Jack London, Mary Austin, Harry Leon Wilson, Upton Sinclair, Nora May French, James Hopper, even (briefly) the young Sinclair Lewis. It was natural, then, that Smith—living in Auburn in the Sierra foothills—should write to Sterling, although Smith no doubt had found much inspiration in Sterling's early cosmic verse. Not long afterward, Sterling paid Smith the high compliment of writing a poem about him: he admitted that "The Coming Singer" was "suggested by *you*" (Sterling to Smith, 22 March 1912). (Amusingly enough, Sterling later included the poem as one of the 100 sonnets he wrote to his lover, Mary Craig Kimbrough, published posthumously as *Sonnets to Craig* [1928].)

Sterling continued to publish substantial volumes of poetry at a regular rate. *The Caged Eagle* (1916), *Thirty-five Sonnets* (1917), and *Sails and Mirage* (1921) had solidified his reputation, at least on the West Coast. He later regretted issuing a collection of war poems, *The Binding of the Beast* (1917), but there are some worthy items even there. And, of course, there are his two scintillating poetic dramas, *Lilith* (1919) and *Rosamund* (1920), the former perhaps his greatest single work. Later poems show Sterling abandoning some of the stiff and archaic diction that had caused much of his early work to seem both antiquated and unauthentic to readers of the 1920s; such gems as "To Life" (in which fantastic imagery underscores the horror and bitterness of existence), the superb atheistic sonnet "To Science," and "The Meteor," with its modified resurrection of cosmic motifs, show that Sterling's poetic vigour was undiminished. Although Henry Holt issued his *Selected Poems* in 1923 and Macmillan published a new edition of *Lilith* in 1926, with a preface by Theodore Dreiser, Sterling's poetic star was inevitably falling: his work simply was not in conformity with the imagistic, free-verse poetry of the Modernists, and he became increasingly embittered by his failure to gain national renown.[4] Life for him had become an endless sequence of alcohol and women, as testified in a letter to H. L. Mencken: "I did more screwing and less drinking in 1925 than in 1924. Even at that I had over a thousand drinks."[5] It is scarcely a surprise that, when he found the effects of alcohol too onerous for his physique

---

4. See Sterling to H. L. Mencken, 7 June 1922: "I've just signed the contract with Holt & Co. for my book of selected poems. [Robert Cortes] Holliday thought that 'Selected Poems' isn't a 'striking title,' so I've suggested 'Neglected Poems' to him." In *From Baltimore to Bohemia: The Letters of H. L. Mencken and George Sterling*, ed. S. T. Joshi (Rutherford, NJ: Fairleigh Dickinson University Press, 2001), p. 163.

5. Sterling to Mencken, 6 January 1926; in *From Baltimore to Bohemia*, p. 224.

to bear, he took his own life in late 1926 by swallowing the vial of cyanide he always kept about him for that purpose.

Sterling was by no means merely a West Coast phenomenon. He had published in many of the leading magazines of the day—the *Nation*, the *Saturday Review*, the *Century Magazine*, *Scribner's Magazine*, Mencken's *Smart Set*, and others. To be sure, he also kept the San Francisco newspapers well stocked with his verse, as well as such little magazines as *All's Well* (run by his colleague Charles J. Finger), the *Reviewer*, the *Sonnet*, *Contemporary Verse*, and such West Coast journals as *Pacific Monthly*, *Lyric West*, and *Sunset*. If he had been a bit more canny in the marketing of his work (Macmillan had wished a collection of new lyrics to follow the republication of *Lilith*, but Sterling never prepared it), he could have achieved a national reputation. His longtime friend Mencken could perhaps have done a bit more toward that end. Although readily publishing dozens of his poems in the *Smart Set* (and a few of his longer ballads in the *American Mercury* in the mid-1920s), Mencken never wrote a substantial review of any book of Sterling's work, and a few years after the latter's death he urged his publisher Alfred A. Knopf not to publish a contemplated biography of Sterling: "I don't think it would be worth while to do a biography of George Sterling. His life, after all, was relatively uneventful, and his writings were scarcely important enough to justify dealing with him at length."[6] Both facets of this judgment are questionable, but in 1931 a biography of Sterling might have been a hard sell. Perhaps the ideal sort of biography (exactly what Franklin Walker produced in *The Seacoast of Bohemia* [1966] and what Sterling scholar Richard K. Hughey is now preparing) would feature Sterling as the focus of a vibrant San Francisco literary circle, whose members can all be credited with piquant and distinctive work.

Sterling's poetry is difficult to characterise, especially because much of it remains unpublished. That he retained his devotion to recognised English metres—including that most rigorous of verse forms, the sonnet, of which he is surely one of the twentieth century's masters—is easy to see, even if we would like to have seen him engage in more work of the sort embodied in that evocative ode in semi-free-verse, "To a Girl Dancing." In his later years Sterling experimented frequently with the ballad form (as for example in "The Young Witch"), but in

---

6. H. L. Mencken to Alfred A. Knopf, 15 July 1931; in *Letters of H. L. Mencken*, ed. Guy J. Forgue (New York: Knopf, 1961), p. 332.

these works one sometimes misses the tightness of structure and imagery found in his other verse. Thematically, Sterling focused on the transience and evanescence of humanity in an endless cosmos that seems to have no purpose; and yet, his cosmicism was not of the remote and chilling sort that we find in Clark Ashton Smith or H. P. Lovecraft, but one that fully recognises the depth and sincerity of human emotions in the face of cosmic meaninglessness. Vergil's *lachrymae rerum* ("the tears of things") were an ever-present reality to Sterling—tears evoked by the passing of beauty, by the appalling "waste" of a Nature that seems heedless of human and animal suffering, and most of all by the eternal inscrutability of all entity. Is it any wonder that the theme of self-annihilation recurs with alarming frequency in his work? From the early sonnet "To One Self-Slain" to the poem purportedly found among his papers upon his death, "My Swan Song," Sterling sees in suicide a release from the torments and struggles of human life, so perhaps it is no surprise that he himself took this avenue of escape when he could no longer endure "the Lords of Pain."

But Sterling and his work refuse to die; whether as a colleague of Ambrose Bierce, Clark Ashton Smith, H. L. Mencken, Jack London, and Theodore Dreiser; as the "King of Bohemia" who nurtured a flowering of exotic and substantial literature in his adopted state; or as a poet and dramatist whose work continues to elicit the admiration of a select few, George Sterling is very much alive in a twenty-first century that would seem to be in far greater need of his delicate and ethereal poetry than his own time ever was. His meditations on human transience notwithstanding, Sterling's work is destined to survive as the valued treasure of those individuals, numerous or few as they may be, capable of relishing his poignant evocations of the wonders and terrors of a boundless cosmos.

—S. T. JOSHI

A Note on the Texts

The poems in this volume have been derived, where possible, from the books, magazines, and newspapers in which they originally appeared; the texts have been checked with manuscripts where possible. The poems have been arranged thematically: Section I features Sterling's "cosmic" poems; Section II his poems dealing with weird or fantastic realms; Section III includes a wide array of pensive philosophical poems; Section IV deals with fantastic creatures; Section V shows Sterling mingling fantasy with romance or eroticism; Section VI features poems in which dreams and fancies are the central focus; Section VII includes tributes to friends and colleagues; and Section VIII contains poems displaying horrific imagery. In each section, the poems are arranged chronologically by date of writing (if known) or date of first publication. My commentary seeks to provide bibliographical and other relevant information on the poems.

I have done most of my research at the New York Public Library, the New York University Library, Columbia University Library, the Bancroft Library at the University of California, the Huntington Library, the Stanford University Library, the Library of Congress, and the University of Washington Library. I am grateful to the librarians of these and other institutions for supplying texts and other assistance.

In my work on Sterling, I have greatly benefited from the assistance and advice of Alan Gullette, Richard K. Hughey, and especially David E. Schultz.

S. T. J.

THE THIRST OF SATAN

I.

The Testimony of the Suns

The Testimony of the Suns

To Whom the unceasing suns belong,
And cause is one with consequence,—
To Whose divine inclusive sense
The moan is blended with the song.
                              —AMBROSE BIERCE.

I.

The winter sunset fronts the North. . . .
    The light deserts the quiet sky. . . .
    From their far gates how silently
The stars of evening tremble forth!

Time, to thy sight what peace they share
    On Night's inviolable breast!
    Remote in solitudes of rest,
Afar from human change or care.

Eternity, unto thine eyes
    In war's unrest their legions surge,
    Foam of the cosmic tides that urge
The battle of contending skies,

The war whose waves of onslaught, met
    Where night's abysses storm afar,
    Break on the high, tremendous bar
Athwart that central ocean set—

From seas whose cyclic ebb and sweep,
    Unseen to Life's oblivious hours,
    Are ostent of the changeless Pow'rs
That hold dominion of the Deep.

O armies of eternal night,
    How flame your guidons on the dark!
    Silent we turn from Time to hark
What final Orders sway your might.

Cold from colossal ramparts gleam,
    At their insuperable posts,
    The seven princes of the hosts
Who guard the holy North supreme;

Who watch the phalanxes remote
    That, gathered in opposing skies,
    Far on the southern wastes arise,
Marshalled by flaming Fomalhaut.

Altair, what captains compass thee?
    What foes, Aldebaran, are thine?
    Red with what blood of wars divine
Glows that immortal panoply?

What music from Capella runs?
    How hold the Pleiades their bond?
    How storms the hidden war beyond
Orion's dreadful sword of suns?

When, on what hostile firmament,
    Shall stars unnamed contend our gyre,
    'Mid councils of Boötes' fire,
Or night of Vega's fury spent?

What tidings of the heavenly fray?
    These, as our sages nightward turn
    To gaze within the gulfs where burn
The helms of that sublime array:

Splendors of elemental strife;
    Smit suns that startle back the gloom;
    New light whose tale of stellar doom
Fares to uncomprehending life;

Profounds of fire whose maelstroms froth
    To gathered armies of offense;
    Cohorts unweariable, immense,
And bulks wherewith the Dark is wroth;

Reserves and urgencies of light
    That flame upon the battle's path,
    And allied suns that brave the wrath
Of systems leagued athwart the night;

Menace of silent ranks that sweep
    Unto irrevocable wars,
    And onset of titanic cars
In Armageddons of the Deep!

Deem we their enginery was not,
    Far in the dim, eternal past?
    Deem we eternity at last
Will find their thunders unbegot?

How haste the unresting feet of Change,
    On life's stupendous orbit set!
    She walks a way her blood hath wet,
Yet deems her path untrodden, strange.

By night's immeasurable dome
    She deems her hopes in surety held—
    Lo! from insurgent deeps impelled
The fleeting systems lapse like foam.

Unshared she deems the kindred skies;
    But runic gulf and star proclaim
    (Archival gloom, prophetic flame)
The immutable infinities:

Vague on the night the mist we mark
    That tells where met the random suns:
    In changeless molds of law it runs
To orbs that roam anew the dark,

And unto which the worlds are born,
    Where Life awakes to know again
    The light of stars, caress of rain,
And winds of the forgotten morn.

Lift up, ye everlasting gates
    Whence fare her feet to wars unknown,
    To heights august of Reason's throne,
And heritage of ampler Fates!

When she, the mindless clay no more
    In Lust's or Fear's potential hands,
    Shall range her uncontested lands
Or sister world's befriending shore.

Till lapse her beatific years
    In emperies of art untold,
    The music of her age of gold
Requiting for unnumbered tears;

Till she behold—the visual boon
    Surviving elemental risk—
    The nearing sun's enormous disc,
Blood-red at dusk of sullen noon;

Till her appointed course be run;
    Till on the darkness faint her breath,
    Flown to the silent void, and Death
Sit crowned upon the ashen sun.

Till sun and sun be met at last
    In warfare that annuls the night,
    When sea and mountain start to light,
Pyres of the sacrificial past,

Dim veils of fire, O world! that were
    The stubborn bastions of thy frame,
    And reaches of abysmal flame
Wherein thy spectral oceans stir—

A mist upon the vassal skies
    Gyrant to Betelgeuse—a flare
    Upon the midnights round Altair—
A portent to barbaric eyes.

O dread and strong Eternity!
    Prickt in an instant of thy clime,
    The bubble of Antares' time
Is one with thine unchanging sea.

Ever the star, unstable, frames
    Her transitory throne of fire,
    But in thy sight how soon expire,
How soon recur, the inviolate flames!—

Throbs of the fitful sun that are
    Unto thine amplitude of sight,
    Even as the quick unrest of light
That stirs, to mortal sense, the star.

What silence rules the ghostly hours
 That guard the close of human sleep!
 Aldebaran crowns the western deep;
Belted with suns Orion tow'rs,

And greaved with light of worlds destroyed,
 And girt with firmamental gloom,
 Abides his far, portended doom
And menace of the warring void.

Shall night allay his high unrest?
 Shall Time his destinies aver,
 Or darkened vastitude deter
His feet from their immortal quest?

Shall augury his goal impart,
 Or mind his hidden steps retrace
 To mausolean pits of space
Where throbs the Hydra's crimson heart?

Ephemeral, may Life declare
 What quarry from the Lion runs,
 And sway the inexorable suns
Where gape the abysses of his lair?

O Night, what legions serve thy wars!
 Lo! thy terrific battle-line—
 The rayless bulk, the blazing Sign,
The leagued infinity of stars!

Remote they burn whose dread array
    Glows from the dark a dust of fire;
    Unheard the storm of Rigel's ire,
A grain of light Arcturus' day.

Unheard their antiphon of death
    Who gleam Capella's cosmic foes;
    Unseen the war whose causal throes
Perturb gigantic Algol's breath—

Whom from afar we mete and name
    Ere Light and Life their doom fulfill,
    Spawn of the Power whose aeons still
The suns of Taurus armed with flame.

What sound shall pass the gulfs where groan
    Their sullen axles on the night?
    What thunder from the strands of light
Whence Vega glares on worlds unknown?

O Deep whose very silence stuns!
    Where Light is powerless to illume
    Lost in immensities of gloom
That dwarf to motes the flaring suns.

O Night where Time and Sorrow cease!
    Eternal magnitude of dark
    Wherein Aldebaran drifts a spark,
And Sirius is hushed to peace!

O Tides that foam on strands untrod,
    From seas in everlasting prime,
    To light where Life looks forth on Time,
And Pain, unanswered, questions God!

What Power, with inclusive sweep
   And rigor of compelling bars,
   Shall curb the furies of the stars,
And still the troubling of that Deep?

What will shall calm that wrathful sky?
   Crave ye tranquillities of light
   Who stand the sons of war and night?
Behold! the Abyss hath given reply.

Wards of Whose realm shall ye avail
   To loose the tentacles of force
   That drag Arcturus from his course,
And rend the weight of Procyon's mail?

Shall yet your feet essay, unharmed,
   The glare of cosmic leaguers met
   Round stellar strongholds gulfward set,
With night and fire supremely armed?

Shall sun or cycle yet confirm
   Your lordship to the unceded Vast,
   Or human period outlast
The vigil of Capella's term?

Deem ye the Eternal Mind will change
   The throned infinity of law
   That never aeon altered saw
In all the Past's eternal range?

Child of unrest, but fain for peace,
   Life dreams, in her expectant dark,
   Of final things, and waits to hark
Conclusive trumpets crying cease.

She lifts an alien voice to call
    To near Denebola: "O sun!
    A little, and thy day is done,
A little, and the Night is all."

A little, and his rays, far-flown,
    Gleam in the dews upon her grave,
    The storied pomps her epochs gave
A dust within her deserts lone.

Yea! so shall Life on worlds afar
    Muse idly of a cosmic tomb,
    Where now past Alioth the gloom
Stirs not with her awaited star.

Her fate, how stranger than we deem!
    Tho' Faith behold with trusting eyes
    A vision on transmuted skies—
The splendors of the human dream;

To live, tho' Pain and Sorrow cease;
    To reach the high Eternal Heart;
    To know Infinity, nor part;
To find the far Ideal, Peace—

The life of each perfected world
    August archangels chanting praise,
    Deep-ranked in everlasting ways,
With wings of grief and exile furled.

O dream not all the worlds fulfill!
    Unblest, unbidden, save of hope.
    Not for finality the scope
And strength of that unaltered Will.

The eternal Night hath writ in stars
    Denial of the ends ye name;
    Ye stand rebuked by suns who claim
The consummation of her wars.

Constrained to what abysmal pole
    Shall severed armies close their flanks
    To stand with deviated ranks,
Subserving to a final goal?

Shall Godhead dream a transient thing?
    Strives He for that which now He lacks?
    Shall Law's dominion melt as wax
At touch of Hope's irradiant wing?

Are these the towers His hands have wrought?
    Dreams He the dream of end and plan
    Dear to the finity of man,
And shall mutation rule His thought?

What powers throng the pregnant gloom!
    Unseen, the ministers of Law
    Reach from eternity to draw
The suns to predetermined doom.

On Law ye serve with kindred might,
    Atom and world that hold her ways;
    The firefly's mote, the comet's blaze,
Are equal in her perfect sight.

Her bonds compel the Vast where boils
    Intensest Spica's sea of fire;
    Her lips decree the hidden gyre
Of bulks that strain in Algol's toils.

Subject to Law's resistless word,
    Thy hands, O Force! resolve the star,
    And toil, at Alphard's battle-car,
His flaming panoply to gird.

Charged, the immeasured gulfs transmit
    Her mandate to the fonts of life,
    Inciting to the governed strife
Whereby the lethal voids are lit,

With augment of imperious tides
    On vague, illimitable coasts,
    And battle-haze of merging hosts
To which the flare of Vega rides.

"But nay!" ye cry, "we trust her hands
    Induce an unconjectured morn,
    To whose divine fulfillment born,
Her strength irrevocable stands."

O lights by which, far-taught, we trace
    The path of Life from death to death!
    O fanes of her recurrent breath,
And strength of Night's annulling mace!—

Profounds whose silences proclaim
    What realms of mystery and awe!
    Colossal Wraths extolling Law
From unsubverted thrones of flame!—

Suns of the Lyre whose thunders rise
    From chords the eternal Hands have smit!
    Stars of the Sword a moment lit
Ere Life re-name her altered skies!—

Without beginning, aim or end;
　　Supreme, incessant, unbegot;
　　The systems change, but goal is not,
Where the Infinities attend.

Deem ye their armaments confess
　　A source of mutable desire?
　　Think ye He mailed His thought in fire
And called from night and nothingness

And armed for Time their high array?
　　Dream ye Infinity was bent
　　Upon a whim, a drama spent
Within an instant of His day?

Think ye He broke His dream indeed,
　　And rent His deep with fearful Pow'rs,
　　That Man inherit fadeless bow'rs?
Desiring, He would know a need!

Nay! stable His Infinity,
　　Beyond mutation or desire.
　　The visions pass. The worlds expire,
Unfathomed still their mystery.

So hath He dreamt. So stands His night,
　　Wherein the suns abiding range,
　　Dust of the dynasties of change,
And altars of eternal light.

December, 1901.

II.

My sleep was like a summer sky
    That held the music of a lark:
    I waken to the voiceless dark
And life's more silent mystery.

Night with her fleeting hours, how brief
    To watch beyond her vault sublime
    The gyrant systems meting Time,
That holds the timelessness of grief!

How pure the light their legions shed!
    How calm above the crumbling tomb
    Of race and epoch passed to gloom
No ray can pierce nor mortal tread!

What gulfs define the cosmic storm!
    The torrent of Capella's light
    A needle on the nerves of sight
Till Force annul the bonds of form;

Till Alcor vanish from the void
    Wherein the Dragon dares the waste,
    Wherein the spawn of Alioth haste
To ghostly bastions long destroyed.

O nearer dark whence Man descries
    Abyssal lamps that flare and sink!
    Profounds where stellar glories shrink,
Or Betelgeuse relumined flies!

In gloom as dense can Spica grope
 As this that bars the human will?
 Desires as vast her children fill,
Or kindred mystery and hope?

Lo! peaceless, ere the veiling day
 Expand where now Arcturus shines,
 I cry to night's ascendant Signs
The timeless questions of the clay:

Will Life, the bourne eternal crossed,
 Attain the secret of her hours?
 Will Sorrow find atoning Pow'rs,
And Love fare heavenward to her lost?

I lift entreating eyes to see
 Gulf beyond gulf till sight relent,
 Sun beyond sun till Time repent
Its question of Infinity.

Shall voice or vision cross the night
 From glooms where grope the hands of Force,
 On law's inexorable course,
To being's transitory light?

Shall Sirius resolve our fears?
 Shall Vega's Lord command the Lyre
 To scatter from her chords of fire
A music on the mortal years?

Shall Procyon with flaming tongue
 Declare the doom his strength awaits,
 Or Rigel's light reveal the Fates
Whereto his shadowed worlds have sung?

O silence of the changeless dark
    Whence Hope uplifts unwearied eyes!
    O patience of devouring skies
That close on Algol's dying spark!

Enhooved with gloom, the Age stamps down
    The palace-flare of Babylon;
    To night the lords of Ur are gone;
The Tyres of Time put by the crown.

To Death the sons of Life are thrust;
    From night to night the nations pace;
    Empire by empire, race by race,
The generations pass to dust.

Enter, O Life! their place of dread,
    And seek their silence to attain:
    Shall Mystery renounce her reign,
Or darkness render thee thy dead?

Where stirs the energy they knew?
    Joins it the forces undestroyed
    That urge the suns within the void,
And shake the star in evening's dew?

Or sit they girt by laws unknown
    Whereto the senses serve as bars—
    With fire of unrecorded stars
That light a heaven not our own?

The Night inevitable waits
    Till fails the insufficient sun,
    And darkness ends the toil begun
By Chaos and the morning Fates,

And starward drifts the stricken world,
   Lone in unalterable gloom,
   Dead, with a universe for tomb,
Dark, and to vaster darkness whirled.

How dread thy reign, O Silence, there!
   A little, and the deeps are dumb—
   Lo! thine eternal feet are come
Where trod the thunders of Altair.

O ashen bulks that haunt the Vast,
   Beyond the ministry of Light!
   O strong intrenchment of the Night
On charred Antares cold at last!

Eternity! thine awful hands
   Shall blot the Lion from our skies,
   And build thy dark for future eyes
Where now illumed Orion stands.

Forever, infinite of range,
   Unceasing whirls the cosmic storm,
   In changeless gulfs where Force and Form
Renew the mystery of change.

A fleeting moment, to thy sight,
   Lamp of thine altar Alphard burns;
   Aldebaran to dusk returns,
And Betelgeuse is stone and night. . . .

What solitudes of gloom unknown
   Abide, O Sun! thy future ways,
   Ere Light at last a sceptre raise,
Resuming her forsaken throne—

When Law's compulsive angels sweep
    A sun unknown athwart thy path;
    When hands resistless wake the wrath
That smites to flame the boiling Deep!

And sprung from that recurrent storm,
    The youthful world exultant wheels,
    Where slow Eternity anneals
The manacles of Time and Form;

Where dim alchemic powers rebuild,
    To Law's immutable designs,
    The primal, unapparent shrines
With Being's basic mystery filled—

Fanes of the slowly fostered spark
    Whose fire shall light the groping clay
    To Reason's sympathetic day
And refuge from the bestial dark.

Reborn to that selective strife
    And fury of ascendant wars,
    What tidings of the immortal shores?
What covenant from Death, O Life?

When, in what maze of spacial bound,
    Or cryptic glooms that wall the grave,
    Hast heard the secret which we crave
From that inscrutable Profound?

What surety that thy sons attain
    The litten council of thy Lords,
    And thunder of seraphic chords
To music not of Time and Pain?

What whisper from the world new-born
    Recalled thy footsteps to essay
    The far, inevitable way
Lit sunward from thy mists of morn?

Nay! were Oblivion's nightward springs
    So fair to thine enchanted eyes
    That now forgot the message lies
From Mystery's reluctant kings?

Nay! are thy lips forever sealed,
    O thou that stoodst aloof with Death—
    Thou that with unrevealing breath
Hast passed the swords his angels wield?

She standeth mute. She cannot say
    (Ah! dumb to Love's appealing Deep!)
    If Death be suzerain of Sleep,
Or Lethe cross the road to Day.

She cannot say if she in sooth
    Abide Infinity's concern,
    Tho' Time's unanswered altars burn
In question to the final Truth.

And yet from unaccording Fates
    We crave the secret of our tears,
    With trust in the betraying years,
And clamor at relentless gates.

And lost within the glooms that fill
    The Night's primordial realm unknown,
    See Mystery on a vaster throne
And Truth's far face receding still.

Shall yet the fearful answer fare
　　To ancient life supremely wise,
　　By seas that flash on alien eyes
The riven sunlight of Altair?

Athwart the gulfs of mote and mind
　　How vast, to Sense, the shadow falls!
　　She gazes from her proven walls
What deeps unfathomable to find!

Lo! wearied with the fruitless quest
　　Their shores invisible to mark,
　　We turn us to the outer Dark,
And gleaming suns far-manifest.

Night! of the dooms to which they sweep
　　What rumor from the battle's verge,
　　Where sun and sun their chariots urge
To leaguers of the hostile Deep?

O Space and Time and stars at strife,
　　How dreadful your infinity!
　　Shrined by your termless trinity,
How strange, how terrible, is life!

How dark to Being's baffled glance
　　The pits of night and nothingness,
　　Here manacled in Law's duress
The allegiant Pleiades advance!

Behold! her little sight is drawn
　　By Hope's untold, immortal ray;
　　Debarred, she seeks atoning day;
Beyond her gloom she dreams a dawn.

Thy secret, O profound of stars!
    We, born of darkness, dare to seek,
    Adjuring Rigel that he speak
His tidings of the eternal wars.

Capella! past thy lonely light
    What Guardians rule the changeless void?
    What final Eden undestroyed
Where seethe the caldrons of the night?—

Where, on the path of suns far-fled,
    Aldebaran goes forth to doom;
    Where unto night's tremendous tomb
The worlds of Procyon are led.

Ere yet below our sky-line dip
    Thy sun-crowned spars to deeps unknown,
    Ere yet our pharos-light be flown,
Declare thy cosmic port, O Ship!

Arcturus! from the abysses vast
    That hush the Voices of thy strife,
    Has heard a whisper unto Life,
Assuring that she rest at last?

Crave ye a truce, O suns supreme?
    What order shall ye deign to hark,
    Enormous shuttles of the dark!
That weave the Everlasting Dream?

Shall Sirius light the gulfs untrod
    That bar, O Life! thy claimant gaze?
    Shall Betelgeuse attend thy ways,
Or Alphard guide thy feet to God?

Shall lone Antares whisper thee
 His attestation to thy hope,
 Or Alioth aid the souls that grope
Within the Night's infinity?

Dost dream to hold the ghostly heights
 That soar beyond Mutation's reign,
 Or sway the tides of Time and Pain,
Lord of the war Arcturus lights?

Wouldst set the Crown upon thy brow?
 Wouldst still the Scorpion's heart of fire?
 Wouldst tread the arc of Rigel's gyre,
Or greet the God his worlds avow?

Lo! claspt to His atoning breast
 In Whom are woe and wrong made just,
 Why this regression to the dust—
This loss of certitude and rest?

What farce were that in which the soul
 Were summoned to celestial peace,
 And, ere her jubilation cease,
Dismissed to her ancestral goal?

To what emergency concealed,
 Abides the realm we seek to share
 Which to all antecedent pray'r
Eternity hath not revealed?

Hath Vega's night diviner shores?
 Shall Spica with surpassing ray
 Illume her worlds with vaster day
Than that Denebola outpours?

Dim are the laws the sages give,
　　For Science sees in all her lands
　　Illusive twilight, in her hands
The judgments of the Relative.

Obscure the glooms that harbor Truth,
　　And mute the lips from which we crave
　　The guarded secret of the grave—
So soon grown dumb to word and ruth!

But ye, O suns! concede the boon
　　To those whose baffled eyes aspire
　　To search your syllables of fire,
And read Orion's telic rune—

The boon to know that Life abides
　　One with your immortality,
　　One with your changing mystery,
And foam of your eternal tides.

Exalt, Infinity, thy might,
　　Nor deem their decrement to mark.
　　Spread thou their ashes on the dark:
Behold! they leap again to light—

To light that summons Life to wake,
　　And stirred from consummated sleep
　　In matter's unconjectured deep,
From mire to mind the pathway take,

The pathway traced with blood and tears,
　　And dust of all our fathers dead,
　　Whose backward footsteps, wandering, red,
Fade to the mist of nameless years.

How oft, O Life, on worlds forgot,
    Hast thou, in thine unnumbered forms,
    Gone forth to Time's transmuting storms,
And fought till storm and stress were not!

How oft hast striven, hoped, and died,
    And, dying, fared to gracious rest,
    The Night's inevitable guest,
In alien realms unverified!

How oft to Mystery and Time
    Returned, their ancient ways to hold,
    With lips that never yet have told
The tidings of that distant clime—

With little hands that could not keep
    The mighty message of the Night,
    Nor are to Day's appealing sight
The hidden annals of thy sleep.

Dost deem the eternity to come
    The secret will disclose at last
    Whereunto an eternal past
Held lips to revelation dumb?

How vast the gulfs of man's desire!
    Children of Change, we dream to share
    The battle-vigil of Altair,
And watch great Fomalhaut expire;

To live, where darkened suns relume
    Their kingdoms in the abysmal haze—
    Where nearing Night attends the blaze
Of high Antares red with doom;

To hear within the deep of Law
 The Word that moves her causal tides;
 To know what Permanence abides
Beyond the veil the senses draw.

And such the hope that fills thy heart,
 O Life! on some allegiant world
 Round Procyon's throne of thunder whirled
Or poised in Spica's gulf apart.

So dreamt thy sons on worlds destroyed
 Whose dust allures our careless eyes,
 As, lit at last on alien skies,
The meteor melts athwart the void.

So shall thy seed on worlds to be,
 At altars built to suns afar,
 Crave from the silence of the star
Solution of thy mystery;

And crave unanswered, till, denied
 By cosmic gloom and stellar glare,
 The brains are dust that bore the pray'r,
And dust the yearning lips that cried.

February, 1902.

Mystery

Men say that sundered by enormous nights
    Burn star and nearest star.
That where companioned seem the sister lights
    The great abysses are.

So held by Life's unsympathetic dark,
    We press to hidden goals.
From gulfs unshared the friending fires we mark,
    And we are lonely souls—

Your hearts, O friends! beyond their veiling bars,
    Are hidden deep away.
Your faces gleam familiar as the stars,
    And as unknown as they.

Three Sonnets on Oblivion

Dedicated to Mr. Raphael Weill

Oblivion

Her eyes have seen the monoliths of kings
 Upcast like foam of the effacing tide;
 She hath beheld the desert stars deride
The monuments of Power's imaginings—
About their base the wind Assyrian flings
 The dust that throned the satrap in his pride;
 Cambyses and the Memphian pomps abide
As in the flame the moth's presumptuous wings.

There gleams no glory that her hand shall spare,
 Nor any sun whose rays shall cross her night,
  Whose realm enfolds man's empire and its end.
No armor of renown her sword shall dare,
 No council of the gods withstand her might:
  Stricken at last Time's lonely Titans bend.

The Dust Dethroned

Sargon is dust, Semiramis a clod!
 In crypts profaned the moon at midnight peers;
 The owl upon the Sphinx hoots in her ears,
And scant and sere the desert grasses nod
Where once the armies of Assyria trod,
 With younger sunlight splendid on the spears;
 The lichens cling the closer with the years,
And seal the eyelids of the weary god.

Where high the tombs of royal Egypt heave,
    The vulture shadows with arrested wings
    The indecipherable boasts of kings,
        As Arab children hear their mother's cry
And leave in mockery their toy—they leave
        The skull of Pharaoh staring at the sky.

The Night of Gods

Their mouths have drunken the eternal wine—
    The draught that Baal in oblivion sips.
    Unseen about their courts the adder slips,
Unheard the sucklings of the leopard whine;
The toad has found a resting-place divine
    And bloats in stupor between Ammon's lips.
    O Carthage and the unreturning ships,
The fallen pinnacle, the shifting Sign!

Lo! when I hear from voiceless court and fane
    Time's adoration of Eternity—
        The cry of kingdoms past and gods undone—
I stand as one whose feet at noontide gain
    A lonely shore; who feels his soul set free,
        And hears the blind sea chanting to the sun.

Three Sonnets of the Night Skies

I—Aldebaran at Dusk

Thou art the star for which all evening waits—
    O star of peace, come tenderly and soon!
    As for the drowsy and enchanted moon,
She dreams in silver at the eastern gates
Ere yet she brim with light the blue estates
    Abandoned by the eagles of the noon.
    But shine thou swiftly on the darkling dune
And woodlands where the twilight hesitates.

Above that wide and ruby lake to-West
    Wherein the sunset waits reluctantly,
        Stir silently the purple wings of Night.
She stands afar, upholding to her breast,
    As mighty murmurs reach her from the sea,
        Thy lone and everlasting rose of light.

II—The Chariots of Dawn

O Night, is this indeed the morning-star,
    That now with brandished and impatient beam
    On eastern heights of darkness flames supreme,
Or some great captain of the dawn, whose car
Scornful of all thy rear-guard ranks that bar
    His battle, now foreruns the helms that gleam
    Below horizons of dissevering dream,
Who lifts his javelin to his hosts afar?

Now am I minded of some ocean-king
    That in a war of gods has wielded arms,

And still in slumber hears their harness ring
And dreams of isles where golden altars fume,
    Till, mad for irretrievable alarms,
        He passes down the seas to some strange doom.

III—The Huntress of Stars

Tell me, O Night! what horses hale the moon!
    Those of the sun rear now on Syria's day,
    But here the steeds of Artemis delay
At heavenly rivers hidden from the noon,
Or quench their starry thirst at cisterns hewn
    In midnight's deepest sapphire, ere she slay
    The Bull, and hide the Pleiades' dismay,
Or drown Orion in a silver swoon.

Are those the stars, and not their furious eyes,
    That now before her coming chariot glare?
        Is that their nebulous, phantasmal breath
Trailed like a mist upon the winter skies,
        Or vapors from a Titan's pyre of death—
    Far-wafted on the orbit of Altair?

The Evanescent

The wind upon the mountain-side
    Sang to the dew: "My moments fly:
    In yonder valley I must die.
How long thy restless gems abide!"

Low to the bent and laden grass
    There came the whisper of the dew:
    "My lessening hours, how fleet and few!
What months are thine ere thou shalt pass!"

The grass made murmur to the tree:
    "My days a little time are fair;
    But oh! thy brooding years to share—
The centuries that foster thee!"

Ere died the wind the tree had said:
    "O mountain marvellous and strong,
    The aeons of thine age—how long,
When I and all my kin lie dead!"

The mountain spake: "O sea! thy strength
    Forevermore I shall not face.
    At last I sink to thine embrace;
Thy waves await my ramparts' length."

The deep gave moan: "O stars supreme!
    Your eyes shall see me mute in death.
    Before your gaze I fade like breath
Of vapors in a mortal's dream."

Then bore the Void a choral cry,
    Descendent from the starry throng:
    "A little, and our ancient song
Dies at thy throne, Eternity!"

Then, silence on the heavenly Deep,
    Wherein that music sank unheard,
    As shuts the midnight on a word
Said by a dreamer in his sleep.

The Thirst of Satan

In dream I saw the starry disarray
   (That battle-dust of matter's endless war)
   Astir with some huge passing, and afar
Beheld the troubled constellations sway
In winds of insurrection and dismay,
     Till, from that magnitude whose ages are
     But moments in the cycle of the star,
There swept a Shadow on our ghost of day—

A Shape that clutched the deviating earth
     And checked its headlong flight and held it fast,
        Draining the bitter oceans one by one.
Then, to the laughter of infernal mirth,
     The ruined chalice droned athwart the Vast,
        Hurled in the face of the offended sun.

Satan, yawning on his brazen seat,
Fondles a screaming thing his fiends have flayed.

The Setting of Antares

The skies are clear, the summer night is old.
The foamless ocean reaches to the West,
    With troubled moonlight on its tranquil breast,
Weary of grief eternally retold.
Now is that hour when winds and waters hold
    A truce of silence and inducing rest,
    And now, like ocean-eagles to their nest,
The stars go seaward, silvery and cold.

Antares, heart of blood, how stir thy wings
Above the sea's mysterious murmurings!
    The road of death leads outward to thy light,
        And thou art symbol for a time of him
            Whose fated star, companionless and dim,
Sinks to the wide horizon of the Night.

Outward

Men say the Janic moon shows but one face,
    Watching our planet with mysterious eyes;
      She turns another gaze on outer skies—
Forever given to the cold of space
And rigor of the frozen dark's embrace.
    Remote, the saber of a comet lies;
      Farther, a pin-point sun in silence dies,
Stilled by the night in its abysmal place.

Other than that she cannot know at all.
    Eternal starlight, desolate and strange,
        Bears to her scrutiny its ghostly sea,
Within whose deeps the systems rise and fall,
      She portion of their toil, and serf to Change—
        One gaze on Time, one on Eternity.

The Face of the Skies

Who shall loose Orion's bands?
    "I!" saith Eternity.
"I with annulling hands
    Shall set the Titan free."

Who shall erect upon the sky
    New forms of might?
Saith Eternity: "I!
    I shall re-people night.

"As a breath on glass,—
    As witch-fires that burn,
The gods and monsters pass,
    Are dust, and return.

"Is the toil much to you
    That is little to me?
Such dreams the gods knew,"
    Saith Eternity.

Ephemera

Unheard but of the spiritual ear,
    Endures the challenge of the timeless Foe—
    Beyond the terrestrial voices and their woe,
An icy music, mercilessly clear.
Ever the sea of Chaos beats more near,
    Nor can one say how soon its tides shall flow
    Above this earth whose transciences we know—
A surf that breaks upon a frozen bier.

However high, however strong we build,
    Abides a higher and a stronger One,
In whose good time the clamorous deeps are stilled
    And the song ended and the labor done.
A little while, their hunger unfulfilled,
    The mothlike worlds flit 'round the guttering sun.

Disillusion

Since boyhood he had loved a certain star,
    And, as the many do, had lifted eyes
    Innocent of the terror of the skies.
Of all the multitude of orbs that are
He chose him one whose pure and icy spar
    Seemed holiest, and when he saw it rise
    Would often whisper: "Make me good and wise!
Lead me to Heaven, O beautiful and far!"

Then he was taken to the silent peak
    Where the astronomers at midnight peer
    On dreadful gulfs, enormous and austere.
He listened, but I did not hear him speak:
    None heard him, stumbling down the mountain, say:
    "A ball of gas! . . . Quadrillion miles away!"

The Meteor

Out of the midnight of the north it came,
 Flung from the sapphire of infinity,
 And soundlessly was buried in the sea—
An orb without a portent or a name.
Only a drowsy helmsman saw its flame,
 A thread of light upon the western Signs—
 Drawn on the darkness where the Bull declines
And Aries trembles at the Hunter's aim.

From deep to deep it passed, with none to know
 What ashes burned upon the caverned skies,—
What altered dust that in the long ago,
  Upon a world now strewn on outer space,
 Gazed in the eyes of love with equal eyes
  Or, for a breath, on their Medusa's face.

The Last Man

Shall that august and uncompanioned one,
    Searching the skies a hundred ages hence,
    Behold upon their solitude the immense
Expiring globe of the defeated sun,
And, knowing that the starry race is run,
    Feel on his brow, sad for Time's afterglow,
    The softly falling paces of the snow,
Soundless as lions' feet in Babylon?

Or, shall he, housed below the planet's crust,
    And weary of the mystery of all,
        Gaze on the engines that his brain has planned,
And near to the nirvana of the dust,
    Accept its old compassion, letting fall
        A giant lever from a nerveless hand?

II.

The Gardens of the Sea

The Nile

Low moaning in the shadows of their might,
   I echo all the voices of my dead.
   I call, until their memory be fled,
Thoth and Osiris sepulchred in night,
High Cheops and the Ramses. In my sight
   Arise the ruins of their pomp, stained red
   As by eternal sunset. I am led
To where the seas are mystery and light.

Thus ordered stand thy destinies, O soul!
   Thou callest, ere the lesser vision flee,
Thy cherished fled before thee to the goal
   Far in the shadows of Eternity.
Thou art drawn down to where Death's thunders roll,
   And lost at twilight in a stranger sea.

The Fog Siren

The grey mist veils the deep, the seeming ghost,
　　Forlorn and olden, of the world's lost seas.
　　Veering to fancies of the muffled breeze,
There moans with ocean down the shrouded coast
(Ceaseless, as from the eternal pain and post,
　　And born of woe no mortal may appease)
　　The siren's grieving, that, as daylight flees,
Summons the drowned, a solemn shadow-host.

Then, as the pallid spectres landward creep,
　　Apocalyptic voices haunt the gloom;
We hear, upon the troubling of the deep,
　　The bellow of the Beast drawn down to doom;
And rending all Death's empire in its sweep,
The trumpet's groaning rolls athwart the tomb.

The Sea-Fog

Far from the marble reaches of the foam,
    It wanders, phantom of the grey old sea.
    The night wherein it passes silently
Was once a deeper darkness—even the home
Of the abyss. So might man's spirit roam,
    Revisiting, from realms unknown set free,
    Forsaken haunts of its mortality,
Sad in the changeless starlight of their dome.

So *she* might come; so from the eternal prime
    Where night and sorrowing together cease,
    Pass earthward in that piteous release.
And shall I call her from the tearless clime?
    From dream and light of her abode of peace?
Nay, lest my grieving reach her out of Time!

Darkness

The Night sate weeping in a lonely land;
　　Or ever, in the faithless truce of Grief,
　　Held dumb communion—ominous relief!—
With Mystery and Silence, hard at hand.

Then crept that vast conspiracy to-West;
　　And then came bird-song and the sunlight, born
　　Of that unnoted miracle of morn,
And for my labor in the darkness, rest. . . .

My mind, grown weary with the day—it seemed—
　　Had lingered o'er the poet's lines too long;
　　Or snows of sorrow hid the flowers of song;
For fire and beauty shunned his page, I deemed.

Then music was, and lo! beneath the dome
　　Of Song's high land I wandered. Found at last
　　Were seas and cities of the fabled past,
And faery islands girt with golden foam.

———

Will dawn at last, beyond the mortal years,
　　Reveal the land that now by faith we name,
　　And Music with celestial lips proclaim
The mystery of unrequited tears?

"Sad Sea-Horizons"

I yearn, beside the solemn sea,
　　To pass its calm horizon-line:
　　In vain, O longing soul of mine!
The star it hides is not for thee.

How strong that hunger of the heart
　　For marvels past the haunted bourne
　　Of unfamiliar seas that mourn
The tale immortal to impart

Of loves forlorn and wars unsung,
　　Forgotten tragedies that were
　　Of old upon the sea, and stir
No music on the poet's tongue.

Ghostly, supreme, their voices lift
　　Beyond the purple of all seas;
　　They lure afar the questing breeze,
And call us that we follow swift—

Voices too sweet for moral sense,
　　That waken where the billows surge
　　A little past the lonely verge
Of seas unknown that call us thence.

"O beautiful and far away!"
　　The lips of ocean seem to cry
　　To youth divine that yearns to try
The perils of a distant day.

Star of romance, how far thy goal!
    Remoter than the moons that gleam
    Above the shadow-lands of dream,
Thy futile splendors stir the soul.

And we that seek thee shall not find,
    Nor linger where thy marvels are,
    Elusive as the sea-line far,
And all the secret of the wind.

Sonnets by the Night Sea

I

Surely the dome of unremembered nights
   Was heavy with those stars! The peaceless sea,
   Casting in foam their fallen shafts to me
Makes ancient music to their awful heights.
O quenchless and insuperable lights!
   What life shall meet your gaze and thence go free
   From litten midnights of eternity
To havens open to your final flights?

Abides nor goal nor ultimate of peace,
   Nor lifts a beacon on the cosmic deep
      To guide our wandering world on seas sublime,
Nor any night to grant the soul release,
   Swung as a pendulum from life to sleep,
      From sleep to life, from Timelessness to Time.

II

Now, as I hear upon the caverned night
   The ocean's ceaseless and stupendous dirge,
   And one by one the stars approach its verge,
The deep seems all one prayer, and the light
Of farthest suns but questions for the sight
   Of men who yet may test the Dark, to urge
   Life's portent from the starlight and the surge,
And read the ancient Mystery aright.

Do blinded powers from their darkness seek,
   Through human sight, that secret to attain?
      From fonts how distant is the spirit fed?

And who are we? And is it we who speak
   The Why we utter to the night of pain,
      The Whither to the unresponding dead?

III

Thou seemest inexhaustible, O sea!
   And infinite of nature; yet I know
   That by divine permission could we go
Within thy sealed and silent deeps, and be
Of all thy glooms and treasuries made free,
   The soul at last each marvel would outgrow,
   Till each were vain as festal fires that glow
Beneath the stars' immortal scrutiny.

And were all alien worlds and suns laid bare
Till Mystery their secret should declare,
   The finite soon its utmost would impart,
      And sun nor world at last have power to thrill
   Man's wayward and insatiable heart,
      Which God and all His truth alone can fill.

IV

The wind of night is like an ocean's ghost.
   The deep is greatly troubled. I, alone,
   See the wave shattered and the wave-crest thrown
Where pine and cypress hold their ancient post.
The sounds of war, the trampling of a host,
   Over the borders of the world are blown;
   The feet of armies deathless and unknown
Halt, baffled, at the ramparts of the coast.

Yea! and the Deep is troubled! In this heart
   Are voices of a far and shadowy Sea,
      Above whose wastes no lamp of earth shall gleam.

Farewells are spoken and the ships depart
    For that horizon and its mystery,
        Whose stars tell not if life, or death, is dream.

V

The wind of night is mighty on the deep—
    A presence haunting sea and land again.
        That wind upon the watery waste hath been;
That wind upon the desert soon shall sweep.
O vast and mournful spirit, wherefore keep
    Thy vigil at the fleeting homes of men,
        Who need no voice of thine to tell them when
Is come the hour to labor or to sleep?

From waste to waste thou goest, and art dumb
    Before the morning. Patient in her tree
        The bird awaits until thy strength hath passed,
Forgetting darkness when the day is come.
    With other tidings hast thou burdened me,
        Whom desolations harbor at the last.

The Gardens of the Sea

Beneath the ocean's sapphire lid
    We gazed far down, and who had dreamed,
    Till pure and cold its treasures gleamed,
What lucent jewels there lay hid?—

Opal and jacinth, orb and shell,
    Calice and filament of jade,
    And fonts of malachite inlaid
With lotus and with asphodel,—

Red sparks that give the dolphin pause,
    Lamps of the ocean-elf, and gems
    Long lost from crystal diadems,
And veiled in shrouds of glowing gauze.

Below, the sifted sunlight passed
    To twilight, where the azure blaze
    Of scentless flowers from the haze
About their dim pavilions cast

Betrayed what seemed forgotten pearls,
    As shimmering weeds alert with light
    Enticed the half-reluctant sight
To caverns where the sea-kelp swirls.

Splendid and chill those gardens shone,
    Where sound is not, and tides are winds,—
    Where, fugitive, the naiad finds
Eternal autumn, hushed and lone;

Till one had said that in her bow'rs
    Where mixt the nacres of the dawn,
    That thence the sunset's dyes were drawn,
And there the rainbow sank its tow'rs.

Where gorgeous flowers of chrysoprase
    In songless meadows bared their blooms,
    The deep's unweariable looms
With shifting splendors lured the gaze.

And zoned on iridescent sands,
    Pellucid glories came and went—
    Silver and scarlet madly blent
In living stars and blazoned bands.

Hydras of emerald and blue
    Were part of swaying tapestries
    Whose woof from ivies of the seas
Stole each inquietude of hue.

And in those royal halls lay lost
    The oriflammes and golden oars
    Of argosies from lyric shores—
'Mid glimmering crowns and croziers tost.

And purple poppies vespertine
    Glowed on the weird and sunken ledge,
    Beyond whose rich, vermillion edge
Rose tentacles from shapes unseen—

Undulant bronze and glossy toils
    That shuddered in the lustrous tide
    And forms in restless crimson dyed
That caught the light in stealthy coils. . . .

Far down we gazed, nor dared to dream
What final sorceries would be
When in those gardens of the sea
The lilies of the moon should gleam.

At the Grand Cañon

Thou settest splendors in my sight, O Lord!
    It seems as though a deep-hued sunset falls
    Forever on these Cyclopean walls,—
These battlements where Titan hosts have warred,
And hewn the world with devastating sword,
    And shook with trumpets the eternal halls
    Where seraphim lay hid by bloody palls
And only Hell and Silence were adored.

Lo! the abyss wherein great Satan's wings
    Might gender tempests, and his dragons' breath
    Fume up in pestilence. Beneath the sun
Or starry outposts on terrestrial things,
    Is no such testimony unto Death
    Nor altars builded to Oblivion.

The Last of Sunset

The moon-dawn, breaking on the eastern height
    Washes in silver the forsaken shore;
    Between the day and dark the sea-gulls soar,
And on the sands the foam is ghostly white.
Arcturus burns, the key-star of the night,
    And swept by winds that never blew before
    The harp-chords of the ocean flash and roar,
And seaward now sinks Venus' golden light.

Alone, I watch her beautiful unrest—
The shuddering of her topaz on the west,
    As heaven and earth accept the twilight hush.
    Far fallen on the violascent seas,
    Where ocean gods awhile to sunset crush
    The scarlet grapes of the Hesperides.

Caucasus

The bastions, lonely as the central sea,
    And stained as with the light of dying suns,
      That tower where the Colorado runs,—
The giant domes of the Yosemite,—
The vast Himalayas, graven by the law
    That was a chisel in the hands of Time—
    Seek not in those the dreadful and sublime:
There lie, far off, regions of deeper awe.

It is a land of many an altar-height,
    And each shall mount his own, in that cold hour
      That brings the dark, the victim and the chain,
When the gaunt vultures, falling from the night,
    Find, as of old, Prometheus in their power—
      Fettered to icy pinnacles of pain.

The Caravan

Still, still I see, by dawn or eventide,
    The city of illusion, far away.
    I thought to find it nearer day by day,
But day by day the sands are blank and wide,
And year by year, with hope alone for guide,
    I watch its iris slowly fade to grey,
    And where the journey ends I cannot say,
Nor these strange folk who travel at my side.

Perhaps we shall not reach those distant halls,
On which the sunset or the moonlight falls
    Weirdly and vast, sowing an inner flame. . . .
    Within our evening fire's concealing light,
The talk of where we go and whence we came
    Begins, then dies upon the desert night.

III.

The Muse of the Incommunicable

Memory of the Dead

O thou that walkest with the quiet dead,
    And keepest vigil in the darkness cast
    Around the portals of the ruined past,
What the strange glory set about thy head,

That we, tho' other lands were surely fair,
    Should wander with thee in thy shadow-lands,
    And yearning, grope for unresponsive hands,
And faces vaguer for the twilight there?

For thou art risen from the ghostly sea
    Of tears of many sorrows. Ah! but when
    We turn aside to rest with Joy again,
We pause, we sigh, we wander yet with thee.

The Altar-Flame

I saw a mountain at the close of day,
    Snow-crowned and lonely, where the after-glow
    Lingered, the ghost of sunset, fading slow.
I said, "This is God's altar, and the way
Earthward, of things eternal, even all they
    That see His face." And evening was, and lo!
    I was aware how that inviolate snow
Upheld a fire! As one that in dismay
Views what he deems a mystery, so I
    Stood silent, till, an alien glory grown,
That light broke loose to a remoter sky
    And in its deeper heaven burned alone.
So had the star of evening, fancied nigh,
    Sate for a little that stupendous throne.

Ultima Thule

Alone I watched one twilight-time
    A little cloud go by,
Remote within the fairer clime
    Of sunset's gleaming sky.

So far, so bright, it drifted on
    O'er ocean's azure wall
I could but muse of glories gone,
    In days beyond recall.

Swift, as to dim Hesperides,
    The wind fled on its way;
It whispered to the kindly trees
    And paused, but could not stay.

The evening star at ocean's brink
    Passed seaward with the night.
How pure it burned! I sighed to think
    What eyes would seek its light.

I fain with star and cloud and wind
    Had held elysian quest
And sought all secrets undivined,
    Beyond the mystic West;

But turned me to familiar things,
    A lowlier way to go,
For who shall take their deathless wings,
    Or who their freedom know?

A sense of loss was at my heart,
Of beauty far and strange,
Of deeper joys in lives apart—
And over all, what change!

The Directory

Selective Time! 'mid all the burthened reams
   Toil graves no name thy fretting moth shall spare,
   Even tho' one say, "Behold! my fame, a flare
Remote in alien dusks, forever gleams,
Lingering with the star." For glory seems,
   In sooth, a sunset drowned by glooming air,
   Nor empire may the stellar vigil share—
Gone like the music of forgotten dreams!

Gone! till on worlds that serve a younger star
   Estranged by voids that blot Arcturus' light,
   Or sunder Vega from the bourne of sight,
     Remoter life shall scan in vain the Deep—
Girt with the voiceless skies that hold afar
     Eternal night, sealing the race's sleep.

In Extremis

Till dawn the Winds' insuperable throng
     Passed over like archangels in their might,
     With roar of chariots from their stormy height,
And broken thunder of mysterious song—
By mariner or sentry heard along
     The star-usurping battlements of night—
     And wafture of immeasurable flight,
And high-blown trumpets mutinous and strong.

Till louder on the dreadful dark I heard
     The shrieking of the tempest-tortured tree,
      And deeper on immensity the call
     And tumult of the empire-forging sea;
But near the eternal Peace I lay, nor stirred,
      Knowing the happy dead hear not at all.

Romance

Thou passest, and we know thee not, Romance!
    Thy gaze is backward, and thy heart is fed
    With murmurs and with music of the dead.
Alas, our battle! for the rays that glance
On thy dethroning sword and haughty lance
    Are of forgotten suns and stars long fled;
    Thou weavest phantom roses for thy head,
And ghostly queens in thy dominion dance.

Would we might follow thy returning wings,
    And in thy farthest haven beach our prow—
        Thy dragons conquered and thine oceans crossed—
And find thee standing on the dust of kings,
    A lion at thy side, and on thy brow
        The light of sunsets wonderful and lost!

A Mood

I am grown weary of permitted things
    And weary of the care-emburdened age—
    Of any dusty lore of priest and sage
To which no memory of Arcadia clings;
For subtly in my blood at evening sings
    A madness of the faun—a choric rage
    That makes all earth and sky seem but a cage
In which the spirit pines with cheated wings.

Rather by dusk for Lilith would I wait
    And for a moment's rapture welcome death,
Knowing that I had baffled Time and Fate,
      And feeling on my lips, that died with day
As sense and soul were gathered to a breath,
      The immortal, deadly lips that kissing slay.

The Moth of Time

Lo! this audacious vision of the dust—
    This dream that it hath dreamt! Unresting wings,
    Too strong for Time, too frail for timeless things!
Whence all thy thirst for God, thy piteous lust
For life to be when matter's chain shall rust?
    What pact hast thou with the undying kings,
    Silence and Death? What sibyl's counsellings
Assure thee that the eternal laws are just?

Nay! all thy hopes are nothing to the Night,
    And justice but a figment of thy dream!
      Upon the waste what wide mirages glow,
With hills that shift, and palms that mock the sight,
    And cities on the desert's far extreme—
      Those veils we name, and dare to think we know!

The Muse of the Incommunicable

An echo often have our singers caught,
    And they that bend above the saddened strings;
    One hue of all the hundred on her wings
Our painters render, and our men of thought
In realms mysterious her face have sought
    And glimpsed its marvel in elusive things.
    Her fragrance gathers and her shadow clings
To all the loveliness that man hath wrought.

The wind of lonely places is her wine.
    Still she eludes us, hidden, husht and fleet,
        A star withdrawn, a music in the gloom.
Beauty and death her speechless lips assign,
    Where silence is, and where the surf-loud feet
        Of armies wander on the sands of doom.

"Omnia Exeunt in Mysterium"

I

The stranger in my gates—lo! that am I,
    And what my land of birth I do not know,
    Nor yet the hidden land to which I go.
One may be lord of many ere he die,
And tell of many sorrows in one sigh,
    But know himself he shall not, nor his woe,
    Nor to what sea the tears of wisdom flow,
Nor why one star is taken from the sky.

An urging is upon him evermore,
    And though he bide, his soul is wanderer,
        Scanning the shadows with a sense of haste
Where fade the tracks of all who went before—
    A dim and solitary traveller
        On ways that end in evening and the waste.

II

How dumb the vanished billions who have died!
    With backward gaze conjectural we wait,
    And ere the invading Shadow penetrate,
The echo from a mighty heart that cried
Is made a sole memorial to pride.
    From out that night's inscrutable estate
    A few cold voices wander, desolate
With all that love has lost or grief has sighed.

Slaves, seamen, captains, councillors and kings,
    Gone utterly, save for those echoes far!
        As they before, I tread a forfeit land,

Till the supreme and ancient silence flings
Its pall between the dreamer and the star.
O desert wide! O little grain of sand!

III

As one that knew not of the sea might come
From slender sources of a mountain stream,
And, wending where the sandy shallows gleam
And boulder-strewn the stumbling waters hum
And white with haste the falling torrents drum,
Might stand in darkness at the land's extreme
And stare in doubt, where, ghostly and supreme,
Muffled in mist and night, the sea lay dumb,—

So shalt thou follow life, a downward rill
A-babble as with question and surmise,
To wait at last where no star beaconeth,
And find the midnight desolate and chill,
And face below its indecisive skies
The Consummation, mystery and death.

To One Self-Slain

The door thou chosest, gave it on the night?
   Ever we ask of whoso openeth
   If day or darkness hold the seats of Death;
But if the heavy-lidded dead have sight
Their mouths are loyal to that alien light:
   Amid the Innumerable no one saith
   What waited on the passing of the breath—
Spend not your own: the grave will not requite.

Phantoms and whispers reach us from the dark—
   Mirages vain, mendacities august
      That are but of the living, not the dead.
Nay! though I hunger, I in no wise hark
   The fleeting music scattered with thy dust,
      Nor call thy shadow from the House of Dread.

Three Sonnets on Sleep

I

Upon the skies of slumber dreams have flight,
    And one from gentlest dreams may wake to weep.
    The dark has moons to sway its utmost deep,
And stars that touch the sleeper from their height.
Ere long, though mute and liberative Night
    Thy soul and sorrow in her poppy steep,
    Her flowers the sickle of the dawn shall reap,
In melancholy meadows of the light.

In vain are Lethe's dews upon the brow,
    Except one find them on its farther shore;
    And he alone has enviable rest
Who sought for peace through many tears, and now
    Whose answered heart a rose is richer for,
    In some old graveyard where the robins nest.

II

Life holds a different pact with every man,
    Though to one sea her many streams descend.
    To some she stands a foe, to some a friend,
Devising each her benison or ban;
And one is saint, and one is courtesan;
    One labors, one is idle to the end.
    Of all her children none shall comprehend
Whether she strive in madness or with plan.

But Death has one condition for us all,
    And he that in the pyramid's deep core
Lies with the graven adamant for pall,

In no profounder pit of silence sleeps
Than he who has his grave by some low shore
To which the thunder-bosomed ocean sweeps.

III

Death has the final answer to our cry,
And past our portals of unrest awaits
Responsive to our question of the Fates;
And he who would attain that deep reply
Must seal his ears to other sounds, and die.
What wonder, if before the midnight gates
The searcher of the riddle hesitates,
Uncertain what those ashen lips deny?

What if the hearer with the pleader cease,
And thus the timeless answer come unheard?
So he that sought for truth should find it peace,
In those long silences where none could hark
The mighty, indecipherable Word
That fell unfathomed on the eternal dark.

Illusion

I am alone in this grey shadowland,—
    This world of phantoms I can never know,—
    This throng of seekers wandering to and fro,
Moved by a hidden god's unheard command;
And though we knew the clasp of eye and hand,
    We watchers of the planet's passing show,
    Yet soon the "now" shall be the "long ago,"
And soon the prow shall grate on Lethe's strand.

Bring on the lights, the music and the wine,
    Ere the long silence give our feast to scorn!
    Let us forget all that we dread we are,
And let the mind's unknown horizon shine,
    As the heart graces with mirage of morn
    The night about its lost and lonely star.

Essential Night

Outreach and touch! But lo! thou hast not found!
    Look forth! But what the tidings of thine eyes?
    Taste! But His apple hath not made thee wise,
Nor hast thou heard His music out of sound.
As light by darkness is my spirit bound,
    And on the soul are question and surmise:
    The vision that I take not from the skies,
Shall that await in the awaiting ground?

Why brood the heavens in large indifference?
    And what is all, and this my spirit what?
And what these apparitions of the sense
      That pass through veils unto us blindfold ones,
    In horror of deep darkness lifting not
      For stars nor moon nor the concealing suns?

To Life

Witch and enchantress, I have watched you feed
    Your children from your cup of poison-brew;
    Subtly you mix the venom and the dew,
That drunken, all may follow where you lead,
Thinking a far mirage their nearer need,
    Whose phantom gardens brighten on the view,
    Where compensating waters may renew
The hearts that thirst, the failing feet that bleed.

Such is the power of your deluding wine
I dream I know its magic and design,
    Saying, "So far, no farther, will I sip,
        Ere the draft grow too bitter." Shall there be
    But deepening illusion for the lip,
        And in the dregs a mightier sorcery?

To Science

And if thou slay Him, shall the ghost not rise?
    Yea! if thou conquer Him thine enemy,
    His specter from the dark shall visit thee—
Invincible, necessitous and wise.
The tyrant and mirage of human eyes,
    Exhaled upon the spirit's darkened sea,
    Shares He thy moment of eternity,
Thy truth confronted ever with His lies.

Thy banners gleam a little, and are furled;
    Against thy turrets surge His phantom tow'rs;
        Drugged with His opiates the nations nod,
    Refusing still the beauty of thine hours;
And fragile is thy tenure of this world
        Still haunted by the monstrous ghost of God.

Waste

The pain in Nature's plan
Is well, perhaps, for Man:
The brute's blind agonies—
What good shall they increase?
What Purpose shall she teach,
There on the foodless beach?—
The murre, the broken wing,
Mauled by the breaker's swing.
The horse's hoof is pressed
Deep in the young larks' nest.
The stags with antlers locked,
Perish with thirst long mocked.
The loosened boulder falls
Upon the ants' sunk halls.
Slow dies the stranded whale
Ringed by the sea-gull's wail.
Stung by the blinded snake,
The calf lies in the brake;
The snake, with broken back,
Writhes in the bullock's track.
The wren has died at morn
Upon the locust-thorn—
Impaled upon that spike
By the relentless shrike.
Gasping the fishes die
As the hot stream goes dry,
And in the forest-fire
What fledglings must expire!
Oh! look what way you will,
Torment and horror still

Are loosed on wordless life
In all the monstrous strife.
There is no justice here
Nor any good made clear.
Considering that Scheme,
Well might the muser dream
He saw on baleful skies
The glare of cruel Eyes,
And heard from pole to pole
An idiot Laughter roll.

Amber

"The Bones of Agamemnon are a show!"
    And only yesterday I held in hand
    That fossil resin from the Baltic strand—
The Miocene in mimic afterglow;
And there, distinct from mandible to toe,
    Perfect as on the day when last he crawled,
    An iridescent beetle widely sprawled,
Caught in that golden gum so long ago.

On some fine morning of the perilled Past,
    He had gone forth so bravely (say, alone,
On his adventure), thorny and cuirassed,
    Eager, perhaps, to win a scarab-throne,
    But found a fate not all unlike our own,
Whom custom's pale viscidities hold fast.

The Dweller in Darkness

The cryptic brain, hid in its house of bone,
    Has windows opening on dusk or day,
    Whence the five senses peer, then turn to say
What the mysterious Beyond has shown;
And whether eagle fly and beetle crawl,
    Or the grey thrush sit fluting in her tree,
    Or sea-winds bear the saltness of the sea
To tasting lips, they tell the Master all.
    But the pent heart shall never see the day,
    From womb to dust, from birth to death's dismay.
Whatever joy or pain the world may send,
    It finds no respite in that living grave,
    But, housed in darkness like a blinded slave,
Toils in unending midnight till the end.

Here and Now

Our brotherhood is stranger than we dream,
The ties more sad. Of all the wandering worlds,
This is the only refuge we may know,
A last and only home. In endless time,
This is our humble span of chartered years,—
In dreadful and interminable space,
Our solitary foothold. Here and now,
Let us take thought. Let us appraise this dust,
And know that here and now for us are all,
And know ourselves the shadows that we are—
Shadows, but ah! so swift to hate and harm!
Life's drama is so terrible and long
To those who suffer! Man ignores its end,
Nor ponders on the pathos of his fate
Amid the infinities. We will not gaze.
Our breath of time is given to little things.
Our joy is builded of another's pain.
Blinded we go, nor ever stand to watch
Those vastitudes whose awe should urge us in
On human things as to a lighted hearth
Where all should sit as brothers. Would you love?
Then there the dear one waits. Another world
Shall not be given: it is here and now.
Above, below, beyond, the eternal gulfs
Conserve the death that shall await all life.
The candle glimmers but an hour. The night
Looms in its ancient hunger. Would you know
The tragedy of human love and need?
Gaze on the stars, then on a brother's face!

IV.

The Black Vulture

The Black Vulture

Aloof upon the day's immeasured dome,
    He holds unshared the silence of the sky.
    Far down his bleak, relentless eyes descry
The eagle's empire and the falcon's home—
Far down, the galleons of sunset roam;
    His hazards on the sea of morning lie;
    Serene, he hears the broken tempest sigh
Where cold sierras gleam like scattered foam.

And least of all he holds the human swarm—
    Unwitting now that envious men prepare
        To make their dream and its fulfilment one,
When, poised above the caldrons of the storm,
    Their hearts, contemptuous of death, shall dare
        His roads between the thunder and the sun.

The Sibyl of Dreams

The rose she gathers is invisible,
  But ah! its fragrance on the visioned air—
  The scent of Paphian flowers warm and fair;
The breath of blossoms delicate and chill,
By Dian tended on her vestal hill,
  And soul of that wan orchid of despair
  Found by Persephone, when, unaware,
She bent to pluck, and hell and heaven grew still.

Oh! in what lily's deep and splendid cup
  Shall ever evening dryads hope to find
   So marvellous a nectar of delight—
In valleys of enchantment gathered up
  By hesitating spirits of the wind,
   And borne in rapture to the lips of Night?

The Last Monster

In backward vision, from the primal dusk
I saw them writhe, reptile and hornéd asp,
Lizard and hydra, serpents of the fen,
Abominable. Then the waddling bulks,
With fangs of death emergent from the slime
Primordial, rose to the light of suns.
Thereafter quaked the rank and steaming earth
To tread of mammoths, and the giant bear,
Insatiate, loomed shaggy on the night,
Contending with the tiger for his glut.
Then sprang the apes, malevolent and swift,
Upon the stage of being—part of life
That lived on life. Then a new darkness fell,
Pierced by the moans of mighty shapes that died.
Whereat the sun rose elder and austere,
And mute against the dawn, alert for death,
With engines of destruction left and right,
Scanning the skies stood the last monster, Man.

"That Walk in Darkness"

Not when the sun is captain of the skies,
    Nor when the sapphire-dwelling moon divine
    Arrows with light the battlements of pine,
Roams Lilith, she whom raptures have made wise;
But one shall see her with enchanted eyes
    When starlight makes mysterious her shrine,
    That whoso drinks her beauty's golden wine
Shall lose his hope and need of Paradise.

And though the cruel vision smite him blind,
    Yet more than they who mourn him is he whole
        On whom her sorceries have burst in flood,—
To whom her lips are offered, that he find
    Her kiss a consternation to the soul
        And scarlet trumpets pealing in the blood.

To the Mummy of the Lady Isis

In the Bohemian Club, San Francisco

No bird shall tell thee of the seasons' flight:
    Sealed are thine ears that now no longer list.
    The little veins of temple and of wrist
Are food no more for sleepless love's delight,
And crumbling in the sessions of thy night,
    Pylon and sphinx shall be as fleeting mist.
    Bitter with natron are the lips that kissed,
And shorn of dreams the spirit and the sight.

Ah! dust misused! better to feed the flow'r,
Than grace the revels of an alien hour,
    When babe or lord wake never to caress
        The bosom where unerring Death hath struck
        And milkless breasts that give the ages suck—
Stilled in the slumber that is nothingness.

Witch-Fire

Said the faun to the will-o'-the-wisp:
　　"You are fugitive, far!"
Said the will-o'-the-wisp to the faun:
　　"But more near than the star."

Said the faun to the will-o'-the-wisp:
　　"You are white, you are cold!"
Said the will-o'-the-wisp to the faun:
　　"I am fire to the bold."

Said the faun to the will-o'-the-wisp:
　　"You are fey, you are fair!"
Said the will-o'-the-wisp to the faun:
　　"If I be, have a care!"

It was far on the marsh that she fled;
　　It was far from the dawn.
Now the winds of the morning have found
　　Not her light nor the faun.

Song

I was a sea-god's daughter,
   Born where the dolphin run.
I stared from crimson coral
   Up to a moonlike sun.

I was a dryad's daughter.
   Singing an elfin rune,
I gazed, beside my birth-tree,
   Up to a star-led moon.

I was a witch's daughter,
   With eyes like agate-spar.
I watched, before her grotto,
   The silver-wanded star.

I am a cobbler's daughter,
   Tired ere my toil is done.
I looked through broken windows
   On star and moon and sun.

The Young Witch

1698
(Elder Davenport Speaks)

Cry bravely, O town crier,
    (And ye, young men, beware!)
How Yale Ratchford, the strong smith,
    Is gone God knoweth where!

Yea! the tall smith is gone
    And comes not home again.
Though he had a shrewish wife,
    He was a man among men.

He shall drink no more ale,
    Nor smoke at the tavern door,
Nor sing old songs at his forge,
    And wrestle young men no more.

This he got for being so strong,
    And this for being so bold
As to have in scorn the white witch
    Who slept in her hair of gold.

By the dark pond in the hills
    She lived when her dam died,
With a black cat which minded her,
    And a black dog at her side.

In pinewood and marshy places
    Her low song was sung,
Where long moss is, and toadstools
    The hue of a goblin's tongue.

Where got she her sullen mouth
    And where her swaying form?
Would she live on eggs and apples
    When the blood of men is warm?

All the town people went shy of her
    When the Ratchford baby died.
Folk tell how she laughed that day,
    And no folk say she cried.

Yale Ratchford cut him a switch
    From a hickory at his door,
And he went up among the hills
    To see she laughed no more.

There were whispers of a hanging
    The day that he went forth,
As had been done by holy men
    At Salem in the north.

A bear was shot at Hadlyme
    With fur as soft as silk,
And Goodman Ames of Saybrook
    Found minnows in the milk.

That night the geese went over,
    A-belling for the Pole.
Some say it was the dark hounds
    That bay a loosened soul.

But saved, or damned forever,
    He comes back home no more,
And we who searched the witch's house
    Found grass against the door.

His wife is shrill in question,
    As she was shrill ere he left,
For all that she is well-nurtured,
    A saver, and right deft.

Now shall be heard much rumor,
    And talk at the tavern door;
And if a stranger come from Boston,
    They'll tell him o'er and o'er.

It was not wise to go hillward
    With hand shut on a switch:
It is not given to young men
    To rid the land of a witch—

Not with eyes so wide apart,
    And with a face so white!
Not if she wander naked
    By a shrunk moon's light!

What shall he do her of service
    As the strong do for the fair?
Shall he forge her an iron marriage-ring,
    Or shoes for the Devil's mare?

For they ha' gone forever—
    Vanished, as men say true,
In blue sky or blue water
    Or the wind between the two.

Eidolon

Eventless days have left me too serene,
    And little know I of the House of Pain;
    But at the falling of the midnight's rain,
Within that scarlet chancel shall be seen
Her face of adverse marble, chill and keen,
    Whose mystery the worlds implore in vain.
    The sphinx of an intolerable fane,
She drowses as the years go forth to gleam.

Her floor is channeled by the feet of all,
    For all have knelt before her, soon or late.
        A few are made her chosen, they that know
More than her lesser ritual—they whose call
    Is her profounder music, as they wait
        And think (and dread to think) of crypts below.

The Sphinx

Where everlasting sleep has smoothed the frown
    From Pharaoh's brow, she stares across the lands
    That hear no more the voice of his commands,
And feel no more the shadow of his crown.
Deep in Time's sea the kings and captains drown,
    As ages buffet with relentless hands
    Her stony face, and blur with driven sands
The runes that told their miserable renown.

Seeking its goal in vastitudes unsown,
    Mirage ahead and barren dust behind,
    Shifting forever in the desert wind,
        The human caravan forever plods,
Beside whose ancient path she waits alone,
        Watching the death of nations and their gods.

V.

The Naiad's Song

The Haunting

Dear, thou art ever with me. For it seems
    That in all forms of beauty I must trace
    Thine utter loveliness, and find thy grace
In gardens where the drooping lily teems;
Nor may the vision vanish: still it gleams
    In all of sweet and beautiful whose place
    Is with the day; at nightfall, lo! thy face,
A phantom pearl within the gulf of dreams!

I would some hidden twilight held us twain
    Wherein all rapture and nepenthe are;
Where we might lose the memory of Pain,
    And smiling, gaze on Sorrow from afar,
As one long dead, who sees sad Earth again
    From Paradise, and deems her but a star.

The Naiad's Song

Far down, where virgin silence reigns,
    In Jasper evenings of the sea,
    I toss my pearls, I wait for thee.
The sea hath lent me all its stains;
    It is but treasure-house of me.

The corals of the sea have caught
    A titan shell whose fragile dome
    Is crimson o'er mine ocean home—
Mine opal chambers subtly wrought
    In semblance of the shaken foam.

Oh, come! and thou shalt dream with me
    By violet foam at twilight tost
    On strands of ocean islets lost
To prows that seek them wearily,
    O'er seas by questing sunsets crost.

All dreams that Hope hath promised Love,
    All beauty thou hast sought in vain,
    All joy held once and lost again—
These, and the mystery thereof,
    I guard beneath the sundering main.

White Magic

Keep ye her brow with starshine crost
    And bind with ghostly light her hair,
O powers benign, lest I accost
    Song's peaceless angel unaware!

One eve her whisper came to earth,
    As eastward woke a thorny star,
To tell me of her kingdom's worth
    And what her liberations are:

She hath the Edens in her gift
    And songs of sovereignties unborn;
In realms agone her turrets lift,
    Wrought from the purples of the morn.

Where swings to foam the dusky sea,
    She waits with sapphires in her hand
Whose light shall make thy spirit be
    Lost in a still, enchanted land.

Musing, she hears the subtle tunes
    From chords where faery fingers stray—
A rain of pearl from crumbling moons
    Less clear and delicate than they.

The strain we lost and could not find
    Think we her haunted heart forgets?
She weaves it with a troubled wind
    And twilight music that regrets.

Often she stands, unseen, aloof,
  To watch beside an ocean's brink
The gorgeous, evanescent woof
  Cast from the loom of suns that sink.

Often, in eyries of the West,
  She waits a lover from afar—
Frailties of blossom on her breast
  And o'er her brow the evening star.

She stands to greet him unaware,
  Who cannot find her if he seek:
A sigh, a scent of heavenly hair—
  And oh, her breath is on his cheek!

The Golden Past

I

Within the stillness of the crypt he lay—
    The vanquished tyrant, quivering and stark,
    Shackled, alone with anguish and the dark,
And conscious of the immolating day
Swept on him as a tiger on its prey,
    To quench with agonies the vital spark,
    When cruel eyes should gloat and laughters mark
The final shames of the tormented clay.

Astounded by atrocities of pain,
    He broke the offended silence with a moan—
      This offal of the rack and glowing brand—
While, as he strove at the relentless chain
    He shuddered, prostrate, on the salted stone,
      A dungeon-rat fed on his mangled hand.

II

But they, his conqueror and faithless queen,
    Beneath the midnight moon lay arrogant,
    Nor saw her beams on kingly marble slant,—
On jasmine and the crowding roses' sheen,
Nor heard the fingers of the harper glean
    Harvests of sound, not heard the ceaseless chant
    Of voices to their godhood consonant.
For them the naked dancer swayed unseen.

For them there stood no past, nor time to be,
For whom all rapture was a tideless sea
    Wherein they dwelt beyond all sound and sight,
       Without a star to touch them with its ray
       Nor pulse of waves to reach them where they lay,
    Welded in dumb convulsions of delight.

The Revenge

Our sweet, long night of sin
Ended in slumber. On my moving breast
Slowly her small, delightful head found rest
From all the cares therein.

O passionate soft dove!
I, too, drank deep of anodyne and dream,
Lost, lost with you beyond that dim extreme
And shadowland of love.

Some time within my sleep
The night crushed in upon me like a mace.
How soon I woke I know not. On my face
I felt my warm blood creep.

It was a coward's blow—
A coward's trick to bind us where we lay!
Then, on the silence and the newborn day,
His voice rang bleak and slow.

"You, thief, did covet her:
So take her now forever! Thigh to thigh,
Bosom to favorable bosom lie,
That bliss escape no spur!"

His chains at neck and knee
Fasten us closely, lest the lovers shrink.
My wrists are bound, but evening food and drink
Gently he proffers me.

God knows I cannot eat.
Water the flesh demands, and I must quaff.
He gives it with a satiated laugh
    That all in Hell repeat.

And she whose lips were red
Ere that accursed morning of surprise?
I kiss no more the mouth and curded eyes
    Of her a fortnight dead.

To a Girl Dancing

Has the wind called you sister?
Sister to Kypris, who, as the far foam kissed her,
   Rose exquisite and white.
For seeing you, we dream of all swift things
   And of the swallow's flight,—
Of sea-birds drifting on untroubled wings,
And incense swaying at the shrine of kings,
In gossamers of violascent light.
In what Sicilian meadows, cool with dew,
   Ran rosier girls than you,
   With tresses dancing free,
To tell how beautiful the world might be?
   In what high days unborn,
Will sheerer loveliness go forth at morn,
To wave a brief farewell to night's last star?
For you, we envy not the lost and far,
   As now you make our day
As happy and imperial as they.

More than the ripple of grass and waters flowing,—
   More than the panther's grace
Or poppy touched by winds from sunset blowing,
   Your limbs in rapture trace
An evanescent pattern on the sight—
Beauty that lives an instant, to become
A sister beauty and a new delight.
So full you feed the heart that hearts are dumb.
Those little hands set back the hands of time,
Till we remember what the world has dreamed,
   In her own clime,

Of Beauty, and her tides that ebb and flow
Around old islands where her face has gleamed,
The marvellous mirage of long ago.

     Ah! more than voice hath said
     They speak of revels fled—
The alabastine and exultant thighs,
     The vine-encircled head.
The rose-face lifted, lyric, to the skies,
The loins by leaping roses garlanded.
     The sandaled years return,
     The lamps of Eros burn,
     The flowers of Circe nod,
And one may dream of other days and lands,
Of other girls that touch unresting hands—
     Sad sirens of the god,
     To some forgotten tune
Swaying their silvern hips below the moon.
     Dance on, for dreams they are indeed,
     A vision set afar,
But you with warm, immediate beauty plead,
And fragrant is your footfall on our star.

O flesh made music in its ecstasy,
Sing to us ere an end of song shall be!
     Of fair things young and fleet!
     White flower of floating feet!
Be glad! Be glad! for happiness is holy!
Be glad awhile, for on the greensward slowly
     Summer and autumn pass,
     With shadows on the grass,
     Till in the meadow lowly
November's tawny reeds shall sigh "Alas!"
     Dear eyes,

What see you on the azure of the skies?
    Enchanted, eager face,
Seek you young Love in his eternal place?
Round arms upflung, what is it you would clasp—
    What far-off lover?
    Hands that a moment hover,
What hands unseen evade awhile your grasp?
Ah! that is best: to seek but not to find him,
For found and loved the seasons yet will blind him
    To this true heaven you are—
That moth unworthy of your soul's white star.
Dance on, and dream of better things than he!
Dance on, translating us the mortal's guess
At Beauty and her immortality—
Yourself your flesh-clad art and loveliness.

Dance, for the time comes when the dance is done
    And feet no longer run
On paths of rapture leading from the day.
    Release not now
The vine that you have bound about your brow:
Dance, granting us awhile that we forget
    How morrows but delay,
Yet come as surely as their own regret.
    Through you the Past is ours,
    Through you the Future flow'rs,
In you their dreams and happiness are met.
    Through you we find again
    That birth of bliss and pain,
That thing of joy and tears and hope and laughter
    That men call youth—
    A greater thing than truth,
    A fairer thing than fame
    In songs hereafter,

A miracle, an unreturning flame,
The season for itself alone worth living,
And needing not our patience nor forgiving.

O heart that knows enough, and yet must learn
    The wisdom that we spurn!
    The years at last will teach you:
    May now no whisper reach you
Of noons when pleading of the flutes shall cease
And not for rapture will you beg, but peace.
To-day it seems too harsh that you should know
    How soon the wreaths must go
    And those flower-mating feet
Be gathered, even as flowers, by cruel Time,
    Their flashing rhyme
No more to mingle with the blood's wild beat.
Dance, with no wind to chill your perfect grace,
    Nor shadow on your face,
Nor voice to call to unenduring rest
The limbs delighting and the naked breast.

Flame

Thou art that madness of supreme desire,
    Which lacking, beauty is but dross and clay.
    Within thy veins is all the fire of·day
And all the stars divinity of fire.
Thine are the lips and loins that never tire,
    And thine the bliss that makes my soul dismay.
    Upon thy breast what god at midnight lay,
To make thy flesh the music of his lyre?

Ah! such alone should know thy loveliness!
Ah! such alone should know thy full caress,
    O goddess of intolerable delight!
        I beg of Fate the guerdon and the grace,
        Far beyond death, to know in thine embrace
Eternal rapture in eternal night.

The Stranger

"Who is he that knocks so loudly
    At the western gate?
Tell me, Love." And Love went proudly;
    And the hour was late.

Fell a silence. Love returning,
    Cried, "I fear thy guest!
In his head what eyes are burning!
    Sable is his crest!

"Nay! I dread him! Close thy portal!
    Be that presence banned!
It may be he is not mortal:
    Hazard not his hand!"

"Who is he that knocks so slowly
    At the western gate?
Tell me Grief?" And Grief went lowly;
    And the hour was late.

Came a laughter. Grief cried gladly,
    "Why, O Love! thy sighs?
Wherefore greet the guest so sadly?
    Tender are his eyes!

"On his crest the gloom discloses
    Stars of purest light.
In his hand immortal roses
    Flood the tranquil night."

"Hold the gate, lest the bars be broken!
  Guard, O Life! the locks!
By the words that both have spoken,
  It is Death who knocks!"

VI.

A Wine of Wizardry

The Summer of the Gods

Methought in dream I saw Ulysses bold—
    Lured by strange music to the hidden West—
    Pass onward in that memorable quest
Of islands where the demigods of old
Beyond the portals of Elysium hold
    The twilight and the threnodies of rest.
    Great gleamed the sunset upon ocean's breast
And all those urgent oars cast up its gold.

Hushed are the voices of the mythic dales
    And lost the days whose dawn and eve of yore
Held yet a mystery whose kindly veils
    Fell as a radiance on sea and shore,
    Whose eastward moons and suns departing bore
A glory unto far, intrepid sails.

Nightmare

Departing troubled to her tryst with Sleep,
    The soul, that night, paused doubtful and afraid
    Within the portals and eternal shade
Of his great temple. All the shapes that sweep
Athwart its twilight, from the abysm they keep
    Rose in tremendous menace. She, dismayed,
    Turned to her day in trembling, nor delayed
Her breathless flight from that portentous deep.

But thou, O Death! shalt feign no dream nor dawn,
    Tho' aeons sunder the hermetic tomb,
    And light annul the mausolean gloom—
Nay! tho' contending sun to sun be drawn
      In ruin that the worlds diffused attest
      To watchers round Arcturus, *I shall rest!*

A Wine of Wizardry

"When mountains were stained as with wine
By the dawning of Time, and as wine
Were the seas."   AMBROSE BIERCE.

Without, the battlements of sunset shine,
'Mid domes the sea-winds rear and overwhelm.
Into a crystal cup the dusky wine
I pour, and, musing at so rich a shrine,
I watch the star that haunts its ruddy gloom.
Now Fancy, empress of a purpled realm,
Awakes with brow caressed by poppy-bloom,
And wings in sudden dalliance her flight
To strands where opals of the shattered light
Gleam in the wind-strewn foam, and maidens flee
A little past the striving billows' reach,
Or seek the russet mosses of the sea,
And wrinkled shells that lure along the beach,
And please the heart of Fancy; yet she turns,
Tho' trembling, to a grotto rosy-sparred,
Where wattled monsters redly gape, that guard
A cowled magician peering on the damned
Thro' vials wherein a splendid poison burns,
Sifting Satanic gules athwart his brow.
So Fancy will not gaze with him, and now
She wanders to an iceberg oriflammed
With rayed, auroral guidons of the North—
Wherein hath winter hidden ardent gems
And treasuries of frozen anadems,
Alight with timid sapphires of the snow.
But she would dream of warmer gems, and so

Shapes of men that were
Point, weeping, at tremendous dooms to be.

Ere long her eyes in fastnesses look forth
O'er blue profounds mysterious whence glow
The coals of Tartarus on the moonless air,
As Titans plan to storm Olympus' throne,
'Mid pulse of dungeoned forges down the stunned,
Undominated firmament, and glare
Of Cyclopean furnaces unsunned.

Then hastens she in refuge to a lone,
Immortal garden of the eastern hours,
Where Dawn upon a pansy's breast hath laid
A single tear, and whence the wind hath flown
And left a silence. Far on shadowy tow'rs
Droop blazoned banners, and the woodland shade,
With leafy flames and dyes autumnal hung,
Makes beautiful the twilight of the year.
For this the fays will dance, for elfin cheer,
Within a dell where some mad girl hath flung
A bracelet that the painted lizards fear—
Red pyres of muffled light! Yet Fancy spurns
The revel, and to eastern hazard turns,
And glaring beacons of the Soldan's shores,
When in a Syrian treasure-house she pours,
From caskets rich and amethystine urns,
Dull fires of dusty jewels that have bound
The brows of naked Ashtaroth around.
Or hushed, at fall of some disastrous night,
When sunset, like a crimson throat to hell,
Is cavernous, she marks the seaward flight
Of homing dragons dark upon the West;
Till, drawn by tales the winds of ocean tell,
And mute amid the splendors of her quest,
To some red city of the Djinns she flees
And, lost in palaces of silence, sees

Within a porphyry crypt the murderous light
Of garnet-crusted lamps whereunder sit
Perturbéd men that tremble at a sound,
And ponder words on ghastly vellum writ,
In vipers' blood, to whispers from the night—
Infernal rubrics, sung to Satan's might,
Or chaunted to the Dragon in his gyre.
But she would blot from memory the sight,
And seeks a stainéd twilight of the South,
Where crafty gnomes with scarlet eyes conspire
To quench Aldebaran's affronting fire,
Low sparkling just beyond their cavern's mouth,
Above a wicked queen's unhallowed tomb.
There lichens brown, incredulous of fame,
Whisper to veinéd flowers her body's shame,
'Mid stillness of all pageantries of bloom.
Within, lurk orbs that graven monsters clasp;
Red-embered rubies smolder in the gloom,
Betrayed by lamps that nurse a sullen flame,
And livid roots writhe in the marble's grasp,
As moaning airs invoke the conquered rust
Of lordly helms made equal in the dust.
Without, where baleful cypresses make rich
The bleeding sun's phantasmagoric gules,
Are fungus-tapers of the twilight witch
(Seen by the bat above unfathomed pools)
And tiger-lilies known to silent ghouls,
Whose king hath digged a somber carcanet
And necklaces with fevered opals set.
But Fancy, well affrighted at his gaze,
Flies to a violet headland of the West,
About whose base the sun-lashed billows blaze,
Ending in precious foam their fatal quest,
As far below the deep-hued ocean molds,

With waters' toil and polished pebbles' fret,
The tiny twilight in the jacinth set,
The wintry orb the moonstone-crystal holds,
Snapt coral twigs and winy agates wet,
Translucencies of jasper, and the folds
Of banded onyx, and vermilion breast
Of cinnabar. Anear on orange sands,
With prows of bronze the sea-stained galleys rest,
And swarthy mariners from alien strands
Stare at the red horizon, for their eyes
Behold a beacon burn on evening skies,
As fed with sanguine oils at touch of night.
Forth from that pharos-flame a radiance flies,
To spill in vinous gleams on ruddy decks;
And overside, when leap the startled waves
And crimson bubbles rise from battle-wrecks,
Unresting hydras wrought of bloody light
Dip to the ocean's phosphorescent caves.

So Fancy's carvel seeks an isle afar,
Led by the Scorpion's rubescent star,
Until in templed zones she smiles to see
Black incense glow, and scarlet-bellied snakes
Sway to the tawny flutes of sorcery.
There priestesses in purple robes hold each
A sultry garnet to the sea-linkt sun,
Or, just before the colored morning shakes
A splendor on the ruby-sanded beach,
Cry unto Betelgeuse a mystic word.
But Fancy, amorous of evening, takes
Her flight to groves whence lustrous rivers run,
Thro' hyacinth, a minster wall to gird,
Where, in the hushed cathedral's jeweled gloom,
Ere Faith return, and azure censers fume,

She kneels, in solemn quietude, to mark
The suppliant day from gorgeous oriels float
And altar-lamps immure the deathless spark;
Till, all her dreams made rich with fervent hues,
She goes to watch, beside a lurid moat,
The kingdoms of the afterglow suffuse
A sentinel mountain stationed toward the night—
Whose broken tombs betray their ghastly trust,
Till bloodshot gems stare up like eyes of lust.
And now she knows, at agate portals bright,
How Circe and her poisons have a home,
Carved in one ruby that a Titan lost,
Where icy philters brim with scarlet foam,
'Mid hiss of oils in burnished caldrons tost,
While thickly from her prey his life-tide drips,
In turbid dyes that tinge her torture-dome;
As craftily she gleans her deadly dews,
With gyving spells not Pluto's queen can use,
Or listens to her victim's moan, and sips
Her darkest wine, and smiles with wicked lips.
Nor comes a god with any power to break
The red alembics whence her gleaming broths
Obscenely fume, as asp or adder froths,
To lethal mists whose writhing vapors make
Dim augury, till shapes of men that were
Point, weeping, at tremendous dooms to be,
When pillared pomps and thrones supreme shall stir,
Unstable as the foam-dreams of the sea.

But Fancy still is fugitive, and turns
To caverns where a demon altar burns,
And Satan, yawning on his brazen seat,
Fondles a screaming thing his fiends have flayed,
Ere Lilith come his indolence to greet,

Who leads from hell his whitest queens, arrayed
In chains so heated at their master's fire
That one new-damned had thought their bright attire
Indeed were coral, till the dazzling dance
So terribly that brilliance shall enhance.
But Fancy is unsatisfied, and soon
She seeks the silence of a vaster night,
Where powers of wizardry, with faltering sight
(Whenas the hours creep farthest from the noon)
Seek by the glow-worm's lantern cold and dull
A crimson spider hidden in a skull,
Or search for mottled vines with berries white,
Where waters mutter to the gibbous moon.
There, clothed in cerements of malignant light,
A sick enchantress scans the dark to curse,
Beside a caldron vext with harlots' blood,
The stars of that red Sign which spells her doom.

Then Fancy cleaves the palmy skies adverse
To sunset barriers. By the Ganges' flood
She sees, in her dim temple, Siva loom
And, visioned with the monstrous ruby, glare
On distant twilight where the burning-ghaut
Is lit with glowering pyres that seem the eyes
Of her abhorrent dragon-worms that bear
The pestilence, by Death in darkness wrought.
So Fancy's wings forsake the Asian skies,
And now her heart is curious of halls
In which dead Merlin's prowling ape hath spilt
A vial squat whose scarlet venom crawls
To ciphers bright and terrible, that tell
The sins of demons and the encharneled guilt
That breathes a phantom at whose cry the owl,
Malignly mute above the midnight well,

Is dolorous, and Hecate lifts her cowl
To mutter swift a minatory rune;
And, ere the tomb-thrown echoings have ceased,
The blue-eyed vampire, sated at her feast,
Smiles bloodily against the leprous moon.

But evening now is come, and Fancy folds
Her splendid plumes, nor any longer holds
Adventurous quest o'er stainéd lands and seas—
Fled to a star above the sunset lees,
O'er onyx waters stilled by gorgeous oils
That toward the twilight reach emblazoned coils.
And I, albeit Merlin-sage hath said,
"A vyper lurketh in ye wine-cuppe redde,"
Gaze pensively upon the way she went,
Drink at her font, and smile as one content.

The blue-eyed vampire, sated at her feast,
Smiles bloodily against the leprous moon.

The Apothecary's

Its red and emerald beacons from the night
Draw human moths in melancholy flight,
With beams whose gaudy glories point the way
To safety or destruction—choose who may!
Crystal and powder, oils or tincture clear,
Such the dim sight of man beholds, but here
Await, indisputable in their pow'r,
Great Presences, abiding each his hour;
And for a little price rash man attains
This council of the perils and the pains—
This parliament of death, and brotherhood
Omnipotent for evil and for good.

Venoms of vision, myrrh of splendid swoons,
They wait us past the green and scarlet moons.
Here prisoned rest the tender hands of Peace,
And there an angel at whose bidding cease
The clamors of the tortured sense, the strife
Of nerves confounded in the war of life.
Within this vial pallid Sleep is caught,
In that, the sleep eternal. Here are sought
Such webs as in their agonizing mesh
Draw back from doom the half-reluctant flesh.
There beck the traitor joys to him who buys,
And Death sits panoplied in gorgeous guise.

The dusts of hell, the dews of heavenly sods,
Water of Lethe or the wine of gods,
Purchase who will, but, ere his task begin,
Beware the service that you set the djinn!
Each hath his mercy, each his certain law,
And each his Lord behind the veil of awe;

But ponder well the ministry you crave,
Lest he be final master, you the slave.
Each hath a price, and each a tribute gives
To him who turns from life and him who lives.
If so you win from Pain a swift release,
His face shall haunt you in the house of Peace;
If so from Pain you scorn an anodyne,
Peace shall repay you with a draft divine.
Tho' toil and time be now by them surpast,
Exact the recompense they take at last—
These genii of the vials, wreaking still
Their sorceries on human sense and will.

Under the Rainbow

Behold we now that City of the Sun
    Whose fame the tale of western legend told—
Queen of that realm where chartless rivers run
    On fabled sands of gold?

They seem not of this earth, these shafts of stone
    Born of a wingèd vision and its grace—
Azures and ambers found in dream alone,
    And found for but a space.

For like to these the dome of Xanadu,
    A bubble lifting from enchanted light,
Shone on the wall of that immortal blue
    The poet saw by night.

Surely in cities of another star
    Such waters and empurpled marbles gleam;
Or these the imaginary towers are
    In vistas of a dream.

Not so. For here the hidden soul of man
    Gives to the day his word of the sublime;
Earth's is the given beauty, and the plan
    Of our own place and time.

Nor need we other worlds to show what Art
    Whispers of her perennial domain—
Whispers, till in her chosen builder's heart
    The vision lives again.

Humble, O man! thine ancient heritage:
    See now what temples and what halls thou hast!
In years to come shall be thy Golden Age,
    When this shall be the Past.

Hope draws her iris from untasted wells,
    And on her skies, in prophecy divine,
Serenely with the rainbow's arch foretells
    What domes shall yet be thine.

The Shadow of Nirvana

Hast ever wakened when the dark was deep,
    Nor known thyself, nor where thou wast, nor why?
    Unquestioned then the drowsy soul may lie,
Somewhere between reality and sleep,
Nor feel the tides of Time and matter sweep—
    Held for a little from the clamorous "I",—
    Pure being, freed of memory and its sigh,
Too far in utter peace to smile or weep.

'Tis but a moment's freedom: soon the mind
    Hears the recalling bugle, and the brow
Harbors the old illusion; soon the Wind
        Is on the dust delivered unto dream,
    And I am I again, and Thou art Thou,
        Who then were one in a diviner Scheme.

The Wiser Prophet

All this I dreamt. Shall any deign to hear
The Dreamer? But the night was moonless, I,
Too weary for the vigil, slept at last,
And in my sleep a vision came to me
Whose voices are forgotten. Yet I heard
Words spoken, though I do not know the tongue;
And faces shown, but whose I cannot say,
So far the skies that held them. As from veils
They stared from out the void—black gossamers
That hang beyond the stars. What Spider wove
The net? And has It snared the gods therein?
What fear is this that shakes the stars? Do they,
Then, tremble in their horror as the flies
Trapped in the web? It was no word of theirs
That crossed the gulf to me. The Message ran
Somewhere between Antares and Altair,
To break on Earth like ocean on a beach;
Yet no man heard save me, and I know not
Its meaning; but beyond the dark I felt
A vaster Dark, whose slow, annuling tide
Creeps nearer to the threshold of the race—
Cold and devouring, exigent and dread,
A symbol and a certainty of doom.
A victim bound, silent as I, the world
Seemed waiting, conscious of the thing foretold:
If I foretell, what ears shall welcome it
Or hand be raised except to threaten me?
Life, passing from mirage to final dust,
Would have no cruel tidings of the goal
Awaiting, but would have her hope sustained

By tongues denying her mortality.
She dreams of an Elysium of peace,
Of pleasures made eternal, and her eyes
Would glut them on illusion. Let her dream!
I will be wise, and show the people not
The shadows of the menace I foresee.
Nay, let them dance, and let the sun-duped throng
Make merry with its harlots to the last.

The Oldest Book

Nor seeking shall you find
The red-bound Book of Elves:
It is not on dusty shelves,
Whose books are for the blind.
It is found, sweet friend,
At a journey's start, not end.
It is nowhere and everywhere—
East, West, North, South.
Its leaves stir in the air
From the loved one's mouth,
As breath moves loosened hair.
When our breaths blend
How shall we read, O friend?
In the heart's need,
How shall we fail to read?

Vainly the scholar delves
In the red-bound Book of Elves:
It is not for his eyes—
The grey elves are too wise.
Blank as the snow each page
That opens to the sage.
He is troubled, for he sees
How we two scan those litanies;
He is angry, for he knows
There are gems beneath the snows.
We shall briefly pity him
Who are as seraphim,
Reading those words of flame,
Ever alike, but never found the same.

Not alone shall you read
The red-bound Book of Elves:
Two shall read, and not one,
But those two are ourselves.
But we shall find no need
For taper, lamp, or sun:
Shut eyes, and it is done!
Only the fall of lid
Reveals the tale there hid.
Then in amazing light
Words of iris leap to sight;
Then indeed that untaught art
Burns deeply in the heart.
Shut eyes and see!
Ah! Read with me!

Farm of Fools

Nameless and uninvited,
　　The gipsy princess came,
And now our sleep is haunted
　　And sleep is not the same.
In dreams we follow blindly
　　Her stained, seducing feet
On wizard roads of shadow
　　Where dead and living meet.

At dawn deceived and tempted
　　By her mysterious mirth,
We trade for gold of sunrise
　　Our wingless gold of earth.
Then broken plow and wagon
　　Are not for us to mend,
When, guided by her laughter,
　　We hunt the rainbow's end.

Often we hear by noontide
　　Notes of a far-off horn
And find, with her for comrade,
　　Pan's hoofprints in the corn.
Out of the wild-grape clusters
　　She presses madder wine
Than vintners of the lowland
　　Take from the tended vine.

By night released and scornful,
　　Regretting then our prayers,
We track her shining footsteps
　　Up immaterial stairs,

A way of joyous peril
  Where boyhood's dragons are—
Built of ascending moonlight
  And ending in a star.

The scandal of our neighbors,
  The envy of their young,
We sing on pagan Sundays
  The wastral words she sung,
And gather for our harvest
  Her poppies in the wheat—
Burning with beauty's witch-fire,
  The laurels of defeat.

VII.

The Passing of Bierce

To Edgar Allan Poe

Time, who but jests with sword and sovereignty,
    Confirming these as phantoms in his gloom
    Or bubbles that his arid hours consume,
Shall mold an undeparting light of thee—
A star whereby futurity shall see
    How Song's eventual majesties illume,
    Beyond Augustan pomp or battle-doom,
Her annals of abiding heraldry.

Time, tho' his mordant ages gnaw the crag,
    Shall blot no hue from thy seraphic wings
        Nor vex thy crown and choral glories won,
Albeit the solvents of Oblivion drag
    To dust the sundered sepulchers of kings,
        In desolations splendid with the sun.

To Ambrose Bierce

Master, when worms have had their will of thee,
  And thou art but a voice along the years—
  A star in the companionship of spheres
That are Fame's firmament—may God decree
That song and song's hostilities shall be
  A sword within my hands, a flame that sears
  The liar's mouth that slanders thee, nor fears
The vengeances of Truth's supremacy!

O Fates that on the tomb of greatness dead
  Permit the viper and the toad to bask,
    Lend me your youngest lightnings, and impel
  My spirit as a whirlwind to the task
To char the liar's tongue within his head—
    Like ashes on the adamant of Hell!

The Ashes in the Sea

N. M. F.

Whither, with blue and pleading eyes,—
    Whither, with cheeks that held the light
Of winter's dawn on cloudless skies,
    Evadne, was thy flight?

Such as a sister's was thy brow;
    Thy hair seemed fallen from the moon—
Part of its radiance, as now
    Of shifting tide and dune.

Did Autumn's grieving lure thee hence,
    Or silence ultimate beguile?
Ever our things of consequence
    Awakened but thy smile.

Is it with thee that ocean takes
    A stranger sorrow to its tone?
With thee the star of evening wakes
    More beautiful, more lone?

For wave and hill and sky betray
    A subtle tinge and touch of thee;
Thy shadow lingers in the day,
    Thy voice in winds to be.

Beauty—hast thou discovered her
    By deeper seas no moons control?
What stars have magic now to stir
    Thy swift and wilful soul?

Or may thy heart no more forget
    The grievous world that once was home,
That here, where love awaits thee yet,
        Thou seemest yet to roam?

For most, far-wandering, I guess
    Thy witchery on the haunted mind,
In valleys of thy loneliness,
        Made clean with ocean's wind.

And most thy presence here seems told,
    A waif of elemental deeps,
When, at its vigils unconsoled,
        Some night of winter weeps.

The Coming Singer

The Veil before the mystery of things
    Shall stir for him with iris and with light;
    Chaos shall have no terror in his sight
Nor earth a bond to chafe his urgent wings;
With sandals beaten from the crown of kings
    Shall he tread down the altars of their night,
    And stands with Silence on her breathless height,
To hear what song the star of morning sings.

With perished beauty in his hands as clay,
    Shall he restore futurity its dream.
Behold! his feet shall take a heavenly way
      Of choric silver and of chanting fire,
    Till in his hands unshapen planets gleam,
      'Mid murmurs from the Lion and the Lyre.

The Passing of Bierce

(These lines were written in reply to rumor that Ambrose Bierce, the poet, critic and satirist, died by his own hand.)

Dream you he was afraid to live?
    Dream you he was afraid to die,
    Or that, a suppliant of the sky,
He begged the gods to keep or give?
Not thus the Shadow-maker stood,
    Whose scrutiny dissolved so well
    Our thin mirage of Heaven and Hell—
The doubtful evil, dubious good.

If, drinking at the close of day,
    The staling wine at last displease,
    And, coming to the bitter lees,
One take the sickened lips away,
Who shall demand the Pilgrim keep
    A twilight session with Disgust,
    And know, since revellers cry he must,
A farewell nausea ere he sleep?

Were his a reason to embrace
    The Roman's dignity of death,
    Whose will decreed his final breath,
Determining the time and place,
Be sure his purpose was of pride,
    A matter not of fear but taste,
    When, finding mire upon the waste,
And hating filth, he turned aside.

If now his name be with the dead,
    And, where the gaunt agaves flow'r,
    The vulture and the wolf devour
The lion-heart, the lion-head,
Be sure that head and heart were laid
    In wisdom down, content to die.
    Be sure he faced the Starless Sky
Unduped, unmurmuring, unafraid.

Shelley at Spezia

Within that peacelessness we call the sea
    Abides a peace. O deep, tremendous bed,
    Accept me, least of all the weary dead,
Where midnight merges to infinity!
Bitter and chill has been life's gift to me.
    Now let the suns go dark within this head,
    And Lethe tower and thunder and be fled,
And I at last be nothing, and go free!

All shall be dust beneath the feet of Change,
And the god's smile, inexorably strange,
    Shall be the world's Medusa, as of old,
        And I be but an echo in the Past—
        Unconscious of that age, so sure at last,
    Whose ruby-litten heavens await the Cold.

VIII.

The Rack

The Lords of Pain

The Lords of Pain are mightier by night:
    Swiftly, as darkness closed the dreary day,
    They marshalled whose inimical array
I saw not, conscious only of their might,
As, thro' the hours' intolerable flight
    And swoon recurrent of the spirit, they
    Wrought grievously their will upon the clay,
Till respite of the dawn's delaying light.

Not thus, O Life! would I depart from thee—
    Relinquishing at Agony's command
The lights and shadows of thine empery;
      But so put by the guerdon of the breath
    As one grown weary in a twilight land,
      Whom Music leads to Sleep, and Sleep to Death.

A Dream of Fear

Unseen the ghostly hand that led,
    I walked where all was darkness, save
    What light the moon, half-wasted, gave
Above a city of the dead.

So lone it was, so grey, I deemed
    That death itself was scarce so old;
    The moonlight fell forlorn and cold
On tombs where Time lay dead, it seemed.

Within its gates I heard the sound
    Of winds in cypress-caverns caught
    Of huddling trees that moaned, and sought
To whisper what their roots had found.

Within its gates my soul was led,
    Down nettle-choked and haunted way—
    An atom of the Dark's dismay,
In deaf immensities of dread.

In broken crypts where ghouls had slept
    I saw how muttering devils sate
    (Knowing the final grasp of Fate)
And told grim auguries, and wept.

The night was mad with nameless fear.
    The Powers of Darkness feared the gloom.
    From sentried sky to anxious tomb
Ran messages I bent to hear.

Mine ears were sealed, nor heard I save
    The secret known to Endor's witch—
    Whispered to lemur and to lich
From lips made wiser by the grave.

O'er tarns where spectral vapors flowed
    Antares shook with bloody light,
    And guarded on its haughty flight
The offended fire of Alphard glowed.

The menace of infinity
    Constrained the cavern of the skies.
    I felt the gaze of solemn eyes
In hostile gulfs intent to see;

Gage of whose imminent designs,
    Satanic Armageddon broke,
    Where monstrous vans in blackness spoke
The flight of Evil on the Signs—

Abysmal occultation cast
    By kingdoms of the sunken noon,
    And shadow-shafts that smote the moon
At altars of the cloven Vast!

To worlds that faltered on their way
    Python's intolerable hiss
    Told from the jaws of his abyss
Malign amazement and dismay.

By god or demon undestroyed,
    In malediction sate the stars,
    Concentered from Titanic wars
To cry the judgments of the Void.

Assigned, implacable, supreme,
    The heralds of the Curse came down:
    I felt the eternal bastions' frown;
I saw colossal cerements gleam.

Convoking trumpets shook the gloom.
    Their incommunicable word
    Announced o'er Time's foundations, stirred,
All vasts and covenants of doom.

I saw the light of dreadful fanes,
    I heard enormous valves resound,
    For aeons sealed in crypts profound,
And clangor of ascending chains.

The Rack

In Hell a voice awoke,
And slowly spoke.

"Not for God's vengeance met,
Not for my torment-sweat,
Not for these agonies
Break I our silences:
Behold their pain excelled
By rapture once unheld.

In Earth's benignest land
We wandered hand in hand.
All beauty and all woe
Were hers awhile to know;
All griefs were given her,
And I sole comforter.
Slowly her love awoke
And like a lily broke;
But ah! to me more dear
The roses of the year,
And I would wander far
Below the crimson star.
Slow as the jasmine grows
I won her from her snows,
Telling with word and deed
My hunger and her need,
Till, all the stream unbarred,
Her blood flowed passionward.
Awhile she recked of shame,
And spoke her Saviour's name;
Awhile her saints did call,

Then promised all.

That night there could not be
The Bliss for her and me;
But soon her lord must go
Beyond the flooded Po;
And soon, in steel arrayed
Went forth his cavalcade;
Then turned my Sweet to me
Telling when all could be—
Ah! God of hate! who heard
Her swiftly spoken word?

'Mid unseen flowers a-bloom
We came across the gloom,
But in that garden-close
Was dark, O Death! thy rose;
And ere mad lips caressed
Or breast was hurled to breast,—
Ere broke her last appeal,
I felt his bravos' steel—
O stealthy hounds that crept
Where the low fountains wept!

So fell the eternal night
Upon our lost delight,
And where its horror lies
I think of Paradise;
Yet not as they that crave
The coolness of its wave—
Sweeter than all therein
The sin we could not sin!
Yea! though infernal art
Goad the remorseful heart,
Till primacies of pain

Within this bosom reign,
First of their legion, first,
In that unsated thirst!—
The pang of lips unkissed,
The rack of raptures missed!"

Then on that fury fell
The silences of Hell.

Conspiracy

I had a dream of some great house of stone,
    Not dark, but open to the northern ray.
    Beneath a cold and somber sky it lay,
Soundless and secret, mournful and alone.

It had no prospect save upon the sky—
    Set in a great and old and windy wood.
    Profound its essence seemed, but not of good;
Yet had one asked, none could have answered why.

A single door it had, that faced the east,
    Ponderous, brazen and without a lock.
    I thought, as stubbornly I dared to knock,
That past the sill a cryptic murmur ceased.

And none said "Enter!" yet I entered there,
    And saw that house was all one marble room,
    Austere, and given to the dead, for whom
The walls held chiseled couches, scant and bare.

Arctic, immense, no pillar stayed that hall,
    And from the north the melancholy light
    Sank through translucent windows, vast and white,
On alabaster niche and frozen pall.

Rigid they lay, that session of the dead,
    From whom the hands of Change seemed held a space,
    With folded arms and enigmatic face,
Marmorean, as portion of their bed.

And half I thought that wafts of presence stole
    On the urned air significantly still,
    Upon whose wintry crystal crept a chill
That fell not on the body but the soul.

That air unused, it seemed to crave escape
    From that sad hall, to be a wind again.
    I felt a terror of those tranquil men,
And feared the wisdom of each silent shape.

Whereat I turned, importunate, to win
    My way to life's complacencies once more;
    Which done, behind the safety of the door
Again I heard that muttering begin.

The Hidden Pool

Far in a wildwood dim and great and cool,
    I found a cavern old,
Where grew, above a pure, unfathomed pool,
    A flower of elfin gold.

There, though the night came lone of any lamp,
    Chill on the flower fell
A pallor faint, inimical and damp,
    A halo like in Hell.

Lambent it gleamed within the twilight calm,
    Long fugitive of day—
Malign, I thought, with alien dew and balm,
    A moon of baneful ray.

A breath of attar, fallen from the bloom,
    Made opiate the air,
Like wafture of an undulant perfume,
    Flown from enchanted hair.

A vampire bat, malignant, purple, cold,
    At midnight came to gleam
The honey that each petal would withhold
    From all but the unclean.

Goblin and witch, I dream, have mingled here
    The venom of their blood,
Nightly communing when that flower of fear
    Had broken not the bud.

But, lich or lemur, none remained to note
    The pollen falling chill,
A film on rock or pool, each yellow mote
    Pregnant with hate and ill.

None other bent to watch, within that crypt,
    The troubled water foam,
Nor knew, beyond, what violet ichor dripped
    From wall and hidden dome,

Nor why (though none came there to fail and drown)
    The troubled fountain boiled,
When touched in that dark clarity, deep down,
    A pallid hydra coiled.

What ghoul may come to pluck that flower of doom
    No witch hath rendered clear:
The warden of an unrevealing gloom,
    I watch and wait and fear.

It well may be a Form of death may own
    The twilight for a pall;
Till then I haunt the caverned air alone,
    With quiet under all.

The Death of Circe

Plotting by night her death,
The god rechanted that Aeaean rune,
Till men beheld a vapor dim the moon
    With grey, demoniac breath.

When charm and rune were whole,
He brought that golden one a golden flagon,
Made in the image of a writhing dragon,
    With teeth that clutched the bowl.

He poured vermilion wine
In that pale cup, to god or faun forbid,
Knowing the witch knew not the venom hid
    In that red anodyne.

He gave the witch, who quaffed
And, drinking, dreamt not who had poured for her,
Nor why the cup came redolent of myrrh,
    Nor why her leopard laughed:

Nor felt, from floor to dome,
Her high pavilion quiver on the dark,
Ere, with an augury too dim to mark,
    A quiet lapped her home.

In all her magic craft
There lay no power to warn her to beware
The bitter drop from Lethe mingled there
    Within the traitor draught.

But ere a pang of fright
Could wake, or he be bidden to depart,
There broke a little wound above her heart,
    From which the blood dripped bright.

And heaven and earth grew dim,
While round the throne there gleamed a coral flood,
From her who knew not why the forfeit blood
    Fell lyrical for him.

To a Monk's Skull

You grin as though you finally had guessed
    How well the dice were loaded, even for you.
    Still, some have ended winners, though a few,
And even losers made their casts with zest.
But at the last you ended like the rest—
    On the Great Hazard: what the mortal threw
    The god surpassed. For once the dice fell true
And all the tavern echoed with the jest.

Perhaps you beat, at that, the tricky game:
    You missed the rose, but missed its thorn as well,
        Crouching in shadow as the condor swooped.
You wagered fleeting bliss with lasting flame,
    And though there was no Heaven and no Hell,
        Death was too kind to show that you were duped.

To Pain

Sandalled with morning and with evening star,
    Draw near me, Lady of ascendant pain,
    Whose hair has touched me in the twilight rain,
Whose home is where unchanging faces are.
You wait me where immortal feet have trod,
    And in your voice is music not-to-be,
    And in your eyes the night of mystery,
Old as the silence on the lips of God.

There is no treason in your given word.
    Your love is past all love, all vain delights,
And holy is the music I have heard.
        'Tis not the Cytherean that shall lead
    To stranger seas and unimagined heights,
        Nor stand in flame beside me at my need.

Epilogue: My Swan Song

Has man the right
To die and disappear,
When he has lost the fight?
To sever without fear
The irksome bonds of life,
When he is tired of strife?
May he not seek, if it seems best,
Relief from grief? May he not rest
From labors vain, from hopeless task?
—I do not know; I merely ask.

Or must he carry on
The struggle, till it's done?
Will he be damned, if he,
World-weary, tired and ill,
Deprived of strength and will,
Decides he must be free?
Is punishment awaiting those,
Who quit, before the whistle blows,
Who leave behind unfinished task?
—I do not know; I merely ask.

George Sterling:
An Appreciation

By Clark Ashton Smith

Among the various literary fervors and enthusiasms of my early youth, there are two that have not faded as such things most often fade, but still retain in these latter years a modicum of their "fringing flames of marvel." Unique, and never to be forgotten, was the thrill with which, at the age of thirteen, I discovered for myself the poems of Poe in a grammar-school library; and, despite the objurgations of the librarian, who considered Poe "unwholesome," carried the priceless volume home to revel for enchanted days in its undreamt-of melodies. Here, indeed, was "balm in Gilead," here was a "kind nepenthe." Likewise memorable, and touched with more than the glamour of childhood dreams, was my first reading, two years later, of "A Wine of Wizardry" in the pages of the old *Cosmopolitan*. The poem, with its necromantic music, and splendors as of sunset on jewels and cathedral windows, was veritably all that its title implied; and—to pile marvel upon enchantment—there was the knowledge that it had been written in my own time, by someone who lived little more than a hundred miles away. In the ruck of magazine verse it was a fire-opal of the Titans in a potato bin; and, after finding it, I ransacked all available contemporary periodicals, for verse by George Sterling, to be rewarded, not too frequently, with some marmoreal sonnet or "molten golden" lyric. I am sure that I more than agreed, at the time, with the dictum of Ambrose Bierce, who placed "A Wine of Wizardry" with the best work of Keats, Poe, and Coleridge; and I still hold, in the teeth of our new Didactic School, the protagonists of the "human" and the "vital," that Bierce's judgment will be the ultimate one regarding this poem, as well as Sterling's work in general. Bierce, whose own fine qualities as a poet are mentioned with singular infrequency, was an almost infallible critic.

Several years later—when I was eighteen, to be precise—a few of my own verses were submitted to Sterling for criticism, through the offices of a mutual friend; and his favorable verdict led to a correspondence, and, later, an invitation to visit him in Carmel, where I spent a most idle and most happy month. I like to remember him, pounding abalones on a boulder in the back yard, or mixing pineapple punch (for which I was allowed to purvey the mint from a nearby meadow), or paying a round of matutinal visits among assorted friends. When I think of him as he was then, Charles Warren Stoddard's fine poem comes to mind. I take pleasure in quoting the lines:

TO GEORGE STERLING

"The Angel Israfel, whose heartstrings are a lute,
and who has the sweetest voice of all God's creatures."

Spirit of fire and dew,
Embodied anew.

Vital and virile thy blood—
Thy body a flagon of wine
Almost divine:
Thou art a faun o' the wood,
A sprite o' the flood,
Not of the world understood.

Voice that is heard from afar,
Voice of the soul of a star.
From thy cloud in the azure above
'Tis thy song that awakeneth love—
Love that invites and awe that retards—
Blessed art thou among bards!
My astral is there where thou art,
Soul of my soul, heart of my heart!

Thou in whose sight I am mute,
In whose song I rejoice;

And even as echo fain would I voice
With timbrel and tabor and flute,
With viol and lute,
Something of worth in thy praise—
Delight of my days—
But may not for lack of thy skill—
For the deed take the will:
Unworthy, ill done, incomplete,
This scroll at thy feet.

Always to me, as to others, he was a very gentle and faithful friend, and the kindest of mentors. Perhaps we did not always agree in matters of literary taste; but it is good to remember that our occasional arguments or differences of opinion were never in the least acrimonious. Indeed, how could they have been?—one might quarrel with others, but never with him: which, perhaps, is not the poorest tribute that I can pay to George Sterling. . . . But words are doubly inadequate, when one tries to speak of such a friend; and the best must abide in silence.

Turning today the pages of his many volumes, I, like others who knew him, find it difficult to read them in a mood of dispassionate or abstract criticism. But I am not sure that poetry should ever be read or criticized in a perfectly dispassionate mood. A poem is not a philosophic or scientific thesis, or a problem in Euclid, and the essential "magic" is more than likely to elude one who approaches it, as too many do, in a spirit of cold-blooded logic. After all, poetry is properly understood only by those who love it.

Sterling, I remember, considered "The Testimony of the Suns" his greatest poem. Bierce said of it, that, "written in French and published in Paris, it would have stirred the very stones of the street." In this poem, there are lines that evoke the silence of infinitude, verses in which one hears the crash of gliding planets, verses that are clarioncalls in the immemorial war of suns and systems, and others that are like the cadences of some sidereal requiem, chanted by the seraphim over a world that is "stone and night." One may quote from any page:

How dread thy reign, O Silence, there!
A little, and the deeps are dumb—
Lo, thine eternal feet are come
Where trod the thunders of Altair!

> Crave ye a truce, O suns supreme?
>   What Order shall ye deign to hark,
>   Enormous shuttles of the dark,
> That weave the Everlasting Dream?

In the same volume with "The Testimony of the Suns" is a blank verse poem, "Music," in which the muse Terpsichore was hymned as never before or since:

> Her voice we have a little, but her face
> Is not of our imagining nor time.

Also, there is the gorgeous lyric "To Imagination," and many chryselephantine sonnets, among which "Reincarnation," "War," and "The Haunting" are perhaps the most perfect.

As I have already hinted, I feel a peculiar partiality for "A Wine of Wizardry," the most colorful, exotic, and, in places, macabre, of Sterling's poems. (This, however, is not tantamount to saying that I consider it necessarily his most important achievement.) Few things in literature are more serviceable as a test for determining whether people feel the verbal magic of poetry—or whether they merely comprehend and admire the thought, or philosophic content. It is not a poem for the literal-minded, for those lovers of the essential prose of existence who edit and read our *Saturday Reviews* and *Literary Digests*. In one of the very last letters that he wrote me, Sterling said that no one took the poem seriously any more, "excepting cranks and mental hermits." It is not "vital" poetry, he said, as the word "vital" is used by our self-elected high-brows (which probably, means, that it is lacking in "sex-kick," or throws no light on the labor problem and the increase of moronism). I was unable to agree with him. Personally, I find it impossible to take the "vital" school with any degree of seriousness, and see it only as a phase of materialism and didacticism. The proponents of the utile and the informative should stick to prose—which, to be frank, is all that they achieve, as a rule. Before leaving "A Wine of Wizardry," I wish, for my own pleasure, to quote a favorite passage:

> Within, lurk orbs that graven monsters clasp;
> Red-embered rubies smoulder in the gloom,
> Betrayed by lamps that nurse a sullen flame,
> And livid roots writhe in the marble's grasp,
> As moaning airs invoke the conquered rust

Of lordly helms made equal in the dust.
Without, where baleful cypresses make rich
The bleeding sun's phantasmagoric gules,
Are fungus-tapers of the twilight witch,
Seen by the bat above unfathomed pools,
And tiger-lilies known to silent ghouls,
Whose king hath digged a sombre carcanet
And necklaces with fevered opals set.

No, "A Wine of Wizardry" is not "vital verse." Thank God for *that,* as Benjamin de Casseres would say.

Notable, also, in Sterling's second volume, is the lovely "Tasso to Leonora" and "A Dream of Fear." His third volume, *A House of Orchids,* is compact of poetry; and, if I were to name my favorites, it would be equivalent to quoting almost the entire index. However, the dramatic poem, *Lilith,* is, I believe, the production by which he will be most widely known. One must go back to Swinburne and Shelley to find its equal as a lyric drama. The tragedy and poetry of life are in this strange allegory, and the hero, Tancred, is the mystic analogue of all men. Here, in the conception of Lilith, the eternal and ineluctable Temptress, Sterling verges upon that incommensurable poet, Charles Baudelaire. In scene after scene, one hears the fugue of good and evil, of pleasure and pain, set to chords that are almost Wagnerian. Upon the sordid reality of our fate there falls, time after time, a light that seems to pass through lucent and iridescent gems; and vibrant echoes and reverberant voices cry in smitten music from the profound of environing mystery.

One might go on, to praise and quote indefinitely; but, in a sense, all that I can write or could write seems futile, now that Sterling is "one with that multitude to whom the eternal Night hath said, I am." Anyway, his was not, as Flecker's,

The song of a man who was dead
Ere any had heard of his song.

From the beginning, he had the appreciation and worship of poetry lovers, if not of the crowd or of the critical moguls and pontiffs.

Of his death—a great bereavement to me, as to other friends—I feel that there is really little that need be said. I know that he must have had motives that he felt to be ample and sufficient, and this is enough for me. I am totally incapable of understanding the smug criticism that

I have read or heard on occasion. To me, the popular attitude concerning suicide is merely one more proof of the degeneracy and pusillanimity of the modern world: in a more enlightened age, felo-de-se will be honored again, as it was among the ancients.

In one of Bierce's books is a trenchant article entitled, "The Right to Take One's Self Off." Here is the final paragraph:

"Why do we honor the valiant soldier, sailor, fireman? For obedience to duty? Not at all; that alone—without the peril—seldom elicits remark, never evokes enthusiasm. It is because he faced without flinching the risk of that supreme disaster—or what we feel to be such—death. But look you: the soldier braves the danger of death; the suicide braves death itself! The leader of the forlorn hope may not be struck. The sailor who voluntarily goes down with his ship may be picked up or cast ashore. It is not certain that the wall will topple until the fireman shall have descended with his precious burden. But the suicide—his is the foeman that never missed a mark, his the sea that gives nothing back; the wall that he mounts bears no man's weight. And his, at the end of it all, is the dishonored grave where the wild ass of public opinion

Stamps o'er his head
But cannot break his sleep."

Commentary

This commentary supplies bibliographical and other information on the poems in this volume, focusing on first appearances in magazines and in collections of Sterling's poems. The following abbreviations are used:

AS   *After Sunset* [ed. R. H. Barlow] (San Francisco: John Howell, 1939)

BB   *Beyond the Breakers and Other Poems* (San Francisco: A. M. Robertson, 1914)

CAS   Clark Ashton Smith

CE   *The Caged Eagle and Other Poems* (San Francisco: A. M. Robertson, 1916)

E   *San Francisco Examiner*

GS   George Sterling

HO   *The House of Orchids and Other Poems* (San Francisco: A. M. Robertson, 1911)

SM   *Sails and Mirage and Other Poems* (San Francisco: A. M. Robertson, 1921)

TFS   *Thirty-five Sonnets* (San Francisco: Book Club of California, 1917)

TS   *The Testimony of the Suns and Other Poems* (San Francisco: W. E. Wood, 1903)

WW   *A Wine of Wizardry and Other Poems* (San Francisco: A. M. Robertson, 1909)

The Altar-Flame: In *TS*.

Amber: *Step Ladder* 7, No. 2 (July 1923): 17. The first line is a quotation from Andrew Lang's "Homeric Unity," in his *Poetical Works* (London: Longmans, Green, 1923), 2.6.

The Apothecary's: In *HO;* rpt. *Pacific Monthly* 25, No. 6 (June 1911): 645 (as "At the Apothecary's Shop").

The Ashes in the Sea: In *HO*. A poem on the poet Nora May French (1881–1907), who committed suicide at GS's house in Carmel on 13 November 1907. GS later assisted in the publication of her *Poems* (1910). See also the sonnet "Nora May French" in *WW*.

At the Grand Cañon: *Poetry* 1, No. 3 (December 1912): 76; in *BB* and *TFS;* also in *Sonnets to Craig* (New York: Albert & Charles Boni, 1928). Written in 1911 (see GS to CAS, 5 October 1911: "We stopped over at the Grand Canyon, a terrific spot to which even an ode would be patronizing, and I wrote a *sonnet* to it!"). It was one of the few poems GS published in *Poetry*, the Modernist poetry magazine founded by Harriet Monroe. Monroe wrote a generally hostile review of *BB*, "The Poetry of George Sterling," *Poetry* 7, No. 6 (March 1916): 307–13, and thereafter GS refused to submit anything to the magazine.

The Black Vulture: *Sunset* 24, No. 3 (March 1910): 243 (as "The Condor"); in *HO* and *TFS*. Perhaps GS's most widely reprinted poem, included in such anthologies as Jessie B. Rittenhouse's *The Little Book of Modern Verse* (1917), Marguerite Wilkinson's *New Voices* (1919), Burton Egbert Stevenson's *Home Book of Verse* (3rd ed. 1918), Edwin Markham's *The Book of Poetry* (1927), Mark Van Doren's *American Poets 1630–1930* (1932), John G. Gregg and Barbara T. Gregg's *Best Loved Poems of the American West* (1980), and the Library of America's *American Poetry: The Twentieth Century—Volume 1* (2000).

The Caravan: *Voices* 5, No. 2 (November 1925): 49.

Caucasus: *Wanderer* 2, No. 9 (September 1924): 115. In Greek myth, Prometheus, in punishment for giving fire to human beings, was chained by Zeus to a rock in the Caucasus mountains, where an eagle fed eternally on his liver (which grew back every night). Aeschylus used this legend for his play *Prometheus Bound*.

The Coming Singer: In *BB* and *TFS;* also in *Sonnets to Craig* (New York: Albert & Charles Boni, 1928). A poem that GS expressly wrote as a tribute to CAS; see Introduction.

Conspiracy: In *CE*.

Darkness: In *TS*.

The Death of Circe: *Reviewer* 2, No. 1 (October 1921): 10–11; in *SM*. In line 2, "Aeaean" refers to the island of Aeaea (in Greek, Aiaia), where the enchantress Circe resides (see Homer, *Odyssey* 10).

The Directory: In *TS*.

Disillusion: *Bookman* (New York) 60, No. 4 (December 1924): 429.

A Dream of Fear: In *WW*. For the witch of Endor (l. 26) see 1 Samuel 28:7–25. Bierce wrote to GS (2 May 1909) about the poem: "It has more great lines, in proportion to its length than anything that you have written—which means anything that any one has written. But it has two stanzas [ten and eleven] that I've put into prose as many ways as the number of times that I've tried to make out their meaning. And I've not found anybody that could guess within a mile of their meaning. Maybe you did not intend that anybody should."

The Dweller in Darkness: *American Parade* 1, No. 4 (October 1926): 61.

Eidolon: *Laughing Horse* No. 6 (1923): [18].

Ephemera: *All's Well* 3, No. 2 (January 1923): 5.

Essential Night: In *CE*.

The Evanescent: *Sunset* 26, No. 2 (February 1911): 172D; in *HO*.

The Face of the Skies: In *SM*.

Farm of Fools: In *AS*. An unidentified newspaper clipping of the poem indicates it appeared in the *New Republic*, but this does not appear to be the case.

Flame: In *Poetica Erotica*, ed. T. R. Smith (New York: Boni & Liveright, 1921–22), 2.319.

The Fog Siren: In *TS;* but the poem was quoted in its entirety in Bierce's "Prattle" (*E*, 12 February 1899, and *New York Journal*, 19 February 1899).

The Gardens of the Sea: In *HO;* also *Sunset* 27, No. 1 (July 1911): 69. A poem whose use of recondite words may have influenced CAS.

The Golden Past: In *Poetica Erotica*, ed. T. R. Smith (New York: Boni & Liveright, 1921–22), 2.317. The poem was written around 1912, and GS sent it to Bierce. Bierce (letter to GS, 9 September 1912) replied: "I'd rather not hand 'The Golden Past' to a woman, and I hope you'll never hand it to the public, though it would doubtless delight the followers of Upton Sinclair. The conclusion is a trifle too graphic; you might as well have used 'the shorter and uglier word.'" GS replied (11 September 1912): "I'm sorry that one of those sonnets offended you. I thought it merely frank, though too frank for publication." GS sent six poems to T. R. Smith for *Poetica Erotica,* expecting Smith to select one or two, but Smith published all six. Smith had encouraged CAS to submit something also, but nothing by CAS was published in the anthology.

The Haunting: In *TS.*

Here and Now: Unpublished in GS's lifetime; included in *George Sterling: A Centenary Memoir-Anthology,* ed. Charles Angoff (South Brunswick, NJ: A. S. Barnes & Co. for the Poetry Society of America, 1969). Text based upon the ms. at Dartmouth College.

The Hidden Pool: In *SM;* rpt. *Reviewer* 2, No. 6 (March 1922): 295–96.

Illusion: In *CE.*

In Extremis: *McClure's Magazine* 28, No. 3 (January 1907): 321; in *WW* and *TFS.* GS remarks: "I 'appealed to Caesar' [i.e., Bierce] on my wind-sonnet, 'In Extremis', and he confirmed, as I rather expected, knowing his tastes, my own high opinion of it. He says, 'This, in my judgement, is one of the greatest things that you have written—and you know what I think that to mean. All that I don't like in it is the compound adjectives. Beware of the compound adjective, beloved of the tyro and the "poetess."'" (GS to Jack London, 25 May 1906; ms., Huntington Library). Bierce's original letter does not appear to survive.

The Last Man: *All's Well* 5, No. 12 (December 1925): 12.

The Last Monster: *Smart Set* 41, No. 4 (December 1913): 130; in *BB.*

The Last of Sunset: *Smart Set* 71, No. 2 (June 1923): 5.

The Lords of Pain: In *TS.*

Memory of the Dead: In *TS.*

The Meteor: *Verse* 2, No. 2 (October–November–December 1925): 16.

A Mood: In *WW* and *TFS*. Lilith is a female demon mentioned once in the Old Testament (Isaiah 34:14) and probably derived from Babylonian sources. In the early mediaeval period a tradition developed that she was Adam's first wife.

The Moth of Time: In *A Book of Verses*, ed. J. Torrey Connor (Oakland: Press of Carruth & Carruth Co., 1910), p. [8]; in *HO*.

The Muse of the Incommunicable: *North American Review* 197, No. 2 (February 1913): 234; in *BB* and *TFS*.

My Swan Song: *San Francisco Call and Post* (appearance unlocated). Purportedly found among GS's papers after his death.

Mystery: In *TS*.

The Naiad's Song: *Sunset* 21, No. 6 (October 1908): 497.

Nightmare: In *TS*.

The Nile: In *TS;* but the poem was quoted in its entirety in Bierce's "Prattle" (*E*, 22 January 1899). Thoth is the Egyptian god of the moon and of wisdom; Osiris is the Egyptian god of the underworld, as well as a vegetation god. "High Cheops" refers to the Pharaoh Khufu (r. 2590–2568 B.C.E.), who built the Great Pyramid. "The Ramses" refers to eleven different pharaohs with the name Ramses (or Rameses), the first two in the 19th dynasty (r. 1304–1303 and 1290–1223 B.C.E., respectively), the rest in the 20th dynasty (r. 1192–1075 B.C.E.).

The Oldest Book: *Lyric West* 4, No. 8 (May 1925): 232–33.

"Omnia Exeunt in Mysterium": In *BB* and *TFS*. The title ("all things end in mystery") is from Thomas Aquinas. This is a much-anthologised poem, appearing in Jessie B. Rittenhouse's *The Second Book of Modern Verse* (1919), Caroline Miles Hill's *The World's Great Religious Poetry* (1923), Edwin Markham's *The Book of Poetry* (1927), and other volumes.

Outward: *Sonnet* 2, No. 2 (January–February 1919): 3; *Argonaut* No. 2190 (15 March 1919): 171. "Janic" is Sterling's coinage—an adjectival form of Janus, the Roman two-faced god who looked both forward and backward.

The Passing of Bierce: *Reedy's Mirror* 25, No. 30 (28 July 1916): 491; in *SM*. GS used the phrase "The Shadow Maker" (see l. 5) as the title of his memoir of Bierce in the *American Mercury* (September 1925).

The Rack: *Smart Set* 39, No. 4 (April 1913): 35–36; in *BB*.

The Revenge: *Contemporary Verse* 5, No. 1 (January 1918): 5.

Romance: In *WW* and *TFS*.

"Sad Sea-Horizons": In *TS*.

The Sea-Fog: In *TS*.

The Setting of Antares: *Sonnet* 1, No. 7 (March–April 1918): 2; in *SM*.

The Shadow of Nirvana: In *CE*.

Shelley at Spezia: *Step Ladder* 6, No. 3 (February 1923): 33. Spezia (more properly La Spezia) is a town in northern Italy, located at the Gulf of La Spezia on the Ligurian Sea. Shelley resided there in 1822. He and two friends had gone to Leghorn to meet Leigh Hunt; on their return to La Spezia on 7 July, their boat was caught in a storm and they were drowned. GS also wrote a lengthy "Ode to Shelley" for the centennial of Shelley's death; it appeared in *Scribner's Magazine* (July 1922) and *AS*.

The Sibyl of Dreams: *Pacific Monthly* 23, No. 6 (June 1910): [frontispiece]; in *HO*. "Paphian" is the adjectival form of Paphos, a city in Cyprus where Aphrodite was worshipped.

Song: *Smart Set* 69, No. 2 (October 1922): 2; in *AS*.

Sonnets by the Night Sea: *Pacific Monthly* 24, No. 6 (December 1910): 616 (Sonnets I–III); in *HO* (Sonnets I–III); in *SM* (Sonnets IV–V [misnumbered V–VI]).

The Sphinx: Unpublished; mss. at the Bancroft Library (Berkeley, CA), Harrison Memorial Library (Carmel, CA), Mills College (Oakland, CA), Lilly Library, Indiana University (Bloomington, IN), and State University of New York (Buffalo, NY).

The Stranger: *All's Well* 3, Nos. 3–4 (February–March 1923): 6.

The Summer of the Gods: In *TS*.

The Testimony of the Suns: In *TS*. GS here, as frequently elsewhere, uses the rhyme-scheme (*abba*) made popular by Tennyson. The epigraph is from Bierce's "Invocation," ll. 45–58, in "Prattle" (*E*, 5 July 1888), collected in *Shapes of Clay* (1903) and in *Collected Works* (1909–12), Vol. 4.

"That Walk in Darkness": *International* 8, No. 2 (February 1914): 62; *E* (28 February 1914): 2; in *BB* and *TFS*. The title comes from the celebrated Biblical phrase "the pestilence that walketh in darkness" (Psalms 91:6).

The Thirst of Satan: *International* 8, No. 1 (January 1914): 26; in *BB* and *TFS*.

Three Sonnets of the Night Skies: *Pacific Monthly* 22, No. 6 (December 1909): 609; in *HO* and *TFS*.

Three Sonnets on Oblivion: *Century Magazine* 76, No. 5 (September 1908): 794–95; in *WW* and *TFS*. One of GS's most frequently reprinted poems. Raphael Weill (1835–1920) was a San Francisco businessman, a prominent member of the Jewish community in the city, and a well-known chef. Sargon (fl. c. 2350 B.C.E.) was the founder of the first Semitic dynasty in Mesopotamia. Semiramis was the wife of the Assyrian king Shamsi-Adad IV (r. 823–811 B.C.E.) and queen regnant during the minority of her son, Adadnirari III. Baal is a Canaanite vegetation deity whose worship is condemned in the Old Testament. "Ammon" refers to the Egyptian creator god Amun.

Three Sonnets on Sleep: *Poetry Journal* 4, No. 5 (January 1916): 182–84; in *CE* and *TFS*.

To a Girl Dancing: First published, apparently, in the *San Francisco Bulletin* (late Dec. 1920 or early 1921), but this appearance has not been located. Separately published as a pamphlet (San Francisco: Printed by Edwin and Robert Grabhorn for Albert M. Bender, 1921); in *SM*. The Grabhorn brothers were renowned specialty publishers known for the impeccable quality of their work. Bender was a San Francisco businessman whose patronage assisted both GS and CAS. In line 2, Kypris is a name for Aphrodite, stemming from her worship on the island of Cyprus (see "The Sibyl of Dreams").

To a Monk's Skull: *All's Well* 5, No. 3 (March 1925): 5.

To Ambrose Bierce: In *WW;* also issued as a separate pamphlet (Washington, DC: Neale Publishing Co., 1910; 200 copies). The sonnet was apparently written in late April 1906, just shortly after the San Francisco earthquake of 17 April. Bierce wrote to GS on 11 June: "I have no objection to the publication of that sonnet on me. It may give my enemies a transient feeling that is disagreeable, and if I can do that without taking any trouble in the matter myself it is worth doing. I think they must have renewed their activity, to have provoked you so— got up a new and fascinating lie, probably. Thank you for putting your good right leg into action themward." To which GS replied on July 5: "No, your enemies have not been brewing any new and fascinating lie about you: I had in mind only a remark that you once made to the effect that you expected them to become active in the event of your death." GS wrote three other poems on or to AB: his "Dedication: To Ambrose Bierce" (in *TS*), "To Ambrose Bierce" (in *HO*), and "The Passing of Bierce," included here.

To Edgar Allan Poe: *Sunset* 13, No. 5 (September 1904): 486 (in column, "Books and Writers"); in *WW*. In debating H. L. Mencken's low opinion of Poe's poetry, GS wrote in 1921: "I've just gone over his poems again, and am surprised at the inequality there. It's usually a case of pure gold or pure lead. I'd no memory of his having written so much that was worthless. As you say, he was no maker of 'good phrases,' even at his best. What he did was a harder thing to do: he put over his aesthetic feeling by means of *atmosphere,* which represents hard artistic work instead of the immediate inspiration. Practically all great lines are the whisper of the subconscious mind. One gets them willy-nilly, without effort. Poe, by the more consciously mental process, made himself unique in literature. 'The light that never was on sea nor land' beats windily through, as if from a Beyond, all of his best work." GS to H. L. Mencken, 28 August 1921; in *From Baltimore to Bohemia: The Letters of H. L. Mencken and George Sterling,* ed. S. T. Joshi (Rutherford, NJ: Fairleigh Dickinson University Press, 2001), p. 139.

To Life: *Sonnet* 1, No. 3 (1917): 2; in *TFS* and *SM*.

To One Self-Slain: In *BB* and *TFS*.

To Pain: *Yale Review* 16, No. 2 (January 1927): 260; *San Francisco Water* 7, No. 3 (July 1928): 12.

To Science: *Sonnet* 2, No. 5 (July–August 1919): 1.

To the Mummy of the Lady Isis: In *CE* and *TFS*. Isis, the chief goddess of ancient Egypt, was a goddess of the earth and protector of the dead; she was the sister and wife of Osiris.

Ultima Thule: In *TS*. The Latin title means "Most remote Thule," referring to a land believed by the Greeks to be in an unidentified locale far to the north.

Under the Rainbow: *Sunset* 35, No. 3 (September 1915): 433; *Town Talk* No. 1205 (25 September 1915): 9.

Waste: *All's Well* 2, Nos. 11–12 (October–November 1922): 153.

White Magic: In *HO*.

A Wine of Wizardry: *Cosmopolitan* 43, No. 5 (September 1907): [551–56]; in *WW*. The poem was begun as early as late 1903 and finished in January 1904 (see Introduction). The epigraph is from Bierce's "Geotheos," ll. 26–28. That poem was first published (without title) in "Prattle" (*E*, 5 June 1887), and collected in *Shapes of Clay* (1903) and in *Collected Works* (1909–12), Vol. 4. In the final line, Bierce changed GS's "sigh" to "smile," commenting: "'smile' seems to me infinitely better as a definition of the poet's attitude toward his dreams" (Bierce to GS, 7 September 1907). GS, in deference to Bierce, acceded to the change, but noted: "I made that change from 'smile' to 'sigh' because I noticed I'd just had Circe and the vampire smile, and was afraid of over-working the word. But I think 'smile' is better, and would prefer it to stand, unless you think the above objection is a valid one" (GS to Bierce, 16 September 1907).

The Wiser Prophet: *All's Well* 3, Nos. 5–6 (April–May 1923): 5; in *AS*.

Witch-Fire: *Smart Set* 60, No. 4 (December 1919): 2.

The Young Witch: *Century Magazine* 106, No. 4 (August 1923): 588–91; in *AS*. The poem also appeared in *West Winds: An Anthology of Verse*, by Members of the California Writers Club (1925), and in Edwin Markham's *The Book of Poetry* (1927).

Index of Titles

Index of First Lines

Printed in the United States
1349100002B/16-39